THE MARKET PLACE APOSTLES
THE LIGHT OF THE WORLD

BY

Barrister Favour Victory

The Marketplace Apostles, The light of the World, Copyright © 2016 by Barrister Favour Victory. All Rights Reserved.

All rights reserved. No part of this book may be reproduced in any form or by any electronic or mechanical means including information storage and retrieval systems, without permission in writing from the author. The only exception is by a reviewer, who may quote short excerpts in a review.

DEDICATION

THIS BOOK IS DEDICATED TO THE HOLY SPIRIT AND ALL THE APOSTLES AT THE MARKET PLACE ALL OVER THE WORLD.

ACKNOWLEDGEMENT

I hereby acknowledge the author of this book THE HOLY SPIRIT. I appreciate my wife Mrs. Gloria Victory and our children for their support and encouragement. My workers that were involved in typing the manuscript.

My prayer is God will bless every person that find time to read this book and more especially those that will put in practice what they learnt from this book.

Table of Contents

DEDICATION   3

ACKNOWLEDGEMENT   4

INTRODUCTION   7

CHAPTER ONE   9
WHO ARE THE APOSTLES?   9

CHAPTER TWO   25
ACTIVITES IN THE MARKETPLACE   25

CHAPTER THREE   67
THE ROLES OF THE APOSTLES IN THE MARKET PLACE   67

CHAPTER FOUR   89
WHAT IS LIGHT?   89

CHAPTER FIVE   97
WHAT THE WORLD REPRESENT   97

CHAPTER SIX   113
THE LIGHT OF THE WORLD   113

CHAPTER SEVEN	*133*
ATTRIBUTES OF BECOMING A LIGHT	*133*
CHAPTER EIGHT	*145*
BATTLES BEFORE BECOMING A LIGHT	*145*
CHAPTER NINE	*155*
PREPARING LAY MEN TO BE APOSTLES AT THE MARKET PLACE	*155*
CHAPTER TEN	*169*
THREE THINGS APOSTLES IN THE MARKET PLACE BECOMES TO THE WORLD	*169*
CHAPTER ELEVEN	*189*
REWARD WHEN YOU BECOME A LIGHT	*189*
CHAPTER TWELVE	*195*
PRACTICAL EXAMPLE OF BEING A LIGHT OF THE WORLD	*195*

INTRODUCTION

From the beginning of God's creation major activities have centered upon the market place apostles.

I must say that even Adam was created as a market place apostle, whose first assignment was to name all the animals God created. Remember, this naming ceremony did not take place in the church or the synagogue; it took place in the Garden of Eden, a market place.

The next assignment given to Adam was to maintain the Garden of Eden (market place). As long as Adam worked with God and maintain a fellowship with God, he remained the light to all God's creature.

This sustained fellowship made Adam have dominion over everything God created. However, when the light of God was withdrawn from Adam, he became a prey to the same creature he dominion.

Taking a cue from what happened to Adam we need to understand that every person God created was meant to be a light of the world and the manifestation of this light is dependent upon your relationship with the giver of the light.

We were not born as pastors or ministers depending. However, everyone was born to be an apostle at the market place.

Even those who have taken priesthood as a career also have a function or responsibility at the marketplace. All the activities of the ministers of the gospel do not start at the pulpit and end at the pulpit.

We all have a role to play at the market place. However, if we must shine, and have great impart, our activities must go beyond the church to the marketplace. It is at the marketplace we have the opportunity to confront and subdue the kingdom of darkness.

The prophet Isaiah assents "Arise, shine…Isaiah 60:1-2: The Bible commands us to "Arise!" it is not a choice but a divine order to shine and become the light of the world God expect us to be apostles in the marketplace. Our shinning is not dependent on our personality traits or our material acquisitions. It is dependent on the glory of God upon our lives.

It will be a failure on our own part as apostle in the market place if we don't utilize effectively the glory of God that has risen upon us.

Remember, your shining as light does not depend upon when every circumstances around you is okay and favourable. You have God as a partner to subdue every darkness.

Isaiah 60:2-3 declares "For behold, the darkness shall cover the earth and gross darkness shall arise upon thee and his glory shall be seen upon thee and the gentiles shall come to thy light, and kings to the brightness of thy rising. "

The scripture notes that despite the darkness that may cover the entire world God's glory will still rise upon us as market place apostles to impart the world.

Be ready to fulfill your divine mandate as a marketplace apostle.

Barr. Favour Victory
November, 2016.

CHAPTER ONE

WHO ARE THE APOSTLES?

William Webster dictionary defined an apostle in the following ways:
(a)   One sent on a mission.
(b)   One of an authoritative New Testament group sent out to preach the gospel and made up especially of Christ's 12 original disciples and Paul.
(c)   The first prominent Christian missionary to a region or group.
(d)   An ardent supporter.

In the same dictionary the synonyms (same in meaning) of an apostles are the following; advocate, advocator, exponent, backer, boaster, champion, expounder, espouser, friend gospeler, herald, hierophant, high priest paladin, promoter, proponent, protagonist, supporter, true believer.

In 1 Corinthians 9:2 "If I be not an apostle unto others, yet doubtless I am to you; for the seal of mine apostleship are ye in the Lord," but Paul described himself as an apostle. In that verse he stated that his apostleship is in the lord, meaning he derives his apostleship from the Lord.

Paul did not attend any seminary school or Bible college before he received the seal of apostleship. Paul was a lawyer by profession and became a tentmaker as he preaches the word.

Paul is a typical example of a market place apostles who used his position at any time an opportunity calls for it. In Acts 16:35-38. "And when it was day, the magistrates sent the sergeants, saying, let those men go. And the keeper of the prison told this saying to Paul, the magistrates have sent to let you go: now therefore depart, and go in peace. But Paul said unto them, they have beaten us openly uncondemned, being Romans, and have cast us into prison; and now do they thrust us out privily? nay verily; but let them come themselves and fetch us out. And the sergeants told these words unto the magistrates: and they feared, when they heard that they were Romans."

As a lawyer Paul utilized his knowledge of constitutional law to query the magistrate for violating his fundamental human right. As a Roman citizen, Paul did not quite the bible or scripture, means Paul was not just an apostle but an apostle in the market place.

When Paul was beaten openly, he did not start contesting over his right as a lawyer, but he submitted to the will of God and when God brought him to the market place (prison) his concern first was to discover the will of God for him in that place. Paul first prayed to receive a direction from God but when the direction did not come, he and his colleague entered into praise and worship. While the praise and worship was going on God, the owner of marketplace introduced himself and gave Paul and his colleague the direction to go.

Paul who did not plan to minister in the prison had opportunity to minister in prison warder's house. In *Acts 16:32:* "And they spoke unto him the word of the Lord and to all that were in his house".

The scripture explains that Paul did not bring himself to the market place but it was arranged by God. In *Acts 16:19* "And when her masters saw that the hope of their gains was gone, they caught Paul and Silas and drew them into **the marketplace** unto the rulers".

In the above verse Paul went about doing his ministry work by casting out the evil spirit in a damsel that makes money for her masters. He never knew that God had ordained that act to bring him into the market place. Paul ministered both in prison and in the prison warden's house as we saw in *Acts 16:32*.

Paul ministration in the prison was not planned by him and the ministration in the prison warden's house also was not planned by Paul. He saw himself in the market place, he did not see it as an opportunity to make more money or get more members for his congregation.

Paul realized that every apostle is a man on a mission. The first point to an apostle in the market place is to minister or accomplish the task given to him by God, thereafter he can demand for his rights or reward.

It was when Paul had finished ministering to the people he decided to employ his legal knowledge to demand for his right that has been infringed upon by the magistrate.

An apostle within this context is not a man that wears collar with a title and supervises some churches or ministry. An apostle is not only a man that plants churches both in the city or the rural area.

The context within which the word apostle is used in this book is the simple meaning given to the word "apostle" by Werriam Webster dictionary. It defines an apostle as a true believer or one sent on a mission to preach the word of God.

Paul's experience in *Acts 16* shows that every professional or business man is an apostle to the market place. Paul did not realize it his understanding was to preach in the synagogue but God orchestrated the event that brought him to the market place as an apostle.

If Paul was not sensitive to the leading of the Holy Spirit, he would have missed the opportunity of preaching to the prisoners, prison warden and his family. This is applicable to some of us who had the opportunity to minister to some people we met at the market place.

Remember, left for the prison warden and the other prisoners, nothing would have brought them to the synagogue or where Paul was preaching. That is why Jesus is sending us to where the people are; either where they are living or where they are working.

Sometimes proper ministration to somebody at the working place opens the doors to the work of God to enter his home as we saw in the case of the prison warden in *Act 16*.

If Paul did not preach to him in the prison yard where else would Paul have seen him to preach to him and perhaps both the prison warden and his entire family would have perished.

The salvation of the family of the prison warden have been planned by God, to be executed by Paul but he must minister to the prison warden first at his place of work which is his market place before Paul can have access to the home of the prison warden.

There are families God had ordained that we should be the one to minister to them but the key person is at work with us or our business partner, a client or customer.

The salvation of the family is being delayed because of our refusal, failure or neglects. The salvation which the family should have received is also been delayed or denied.

When Paul was coming to that city, the prison, and prison warden's house was not included in the places he would go to minister.

He saw himself as an apostle meant only for the church or synagogue but God saw Paul as an apostle not only for the church but also for the market place.

With your collar you can still minister at the market place like Paul. Without collar, your place of ministration is your home, office, business arena etc. regarded as the market place.

The story of Andrew is quite explicit as narrated in *John 1:40-41* "One of the two which heard John speak and followed him was

Andrew, Simon Peter's brother. He first findeth his own brother Simon, and saith unto him, we have found the Messiah, which is, being interpreted, the Christ".

Andrew was one of the first to hear from John the Baptist that Jesus is the Messiah. As an apostle in the marketplace, he first of all preached to Peter about Jesus. To the story of Peter as chief apostle of Jesus disciples cannot be complete without mentioning Andrew. There is no other record of Andrew preaching to anybody else but the only fish Andrew's net caught in his house was indeed a big fish both for the kingdom and for his generation.

What makes you an apostle is not dependent upon your title or your position in a local church, ministry or fellowship, what makes you an apostle is dependent upon your functionality in the purpose of God for your life.

Some have left the marketplace, a place of their calling and run into the church to take up a pastoral responsibility because they believe that the call of God was upon their life.

Perhaps Paul wouldn't have ministered to kings and rulers if he did not have *Acts 16* experience. I believe it is the experience of ministering to the prisoner and prison warden that opened his eyes to the call of God upon his life. He became an apostle in the marketplace.

Your belief that God has called you to preach is good but that does not limit you preaching only in the church. The people in the marketplace are among the creatures referred to in **Romans. 8:19** "For the earnest expectation of the creature waiteth for the manifestation of the sons of God". These creatures are waiting for the manifestation of the sons of God.

Are you a son of God? Do you know that all creature are waiting for your manifestation in your office, at home, in the village, in the city, in the neighbourhood, business centres, hospitals, market and other public places.

If you are a son of God found in this places mentioned above and you have refused to be their apostle, can creature consider you to be among the sons of God whose manifestation they are waiting for?

Apostleship is not an issue of title. It is an issue of responsibility and functionality. You cannot be an apostle and you are not active in the place of your calling.

Looking at another meaning of apostle, as defined by the Werriam Webster dictionary can zero in on "friend".

Are you a friend of God? Are you also a friend of Jesus? If you are, it means that you are his friend in marketplace. What do you do for your friend when he expects something from you? ***Proverbs. 17:17*** "A friend loveth at all times." An apostle is also a friend of God at the market place. Jesus said if you love me do my commandments. The last commandment Jesus gave us before he left the world after his resurrection is found in ***Acts 1:8*** "But ye shall receive power, after that the Holy Ghost is come upon you and ye shall be witnesses unto me both in Jerusalem, and in all Judea, and in Samaria, and unto the uttermost part of the earth".

It is a command from our God and friend to be his witnessess. But there is no other place you can witness about God's love, salvation, protection, security, kindness, provision, promotion, healing and deliverance except in the market place, where you work or do business. Apostle's function is not only limited to preaching, it also involves sharing your testimony. When you share the testimony of God's goodness upon your life you are also doing your apostolic function. Every testimony shared with an invitation to receive Christ is indeed an apostolic function.

Remember, what all the pastors in a local church does every Sunday or service day is to share testimonies of people written in the bible about how the word of God brought testimonies to their lives. Thereafter they make an invitation to unbelievers to receive Jesus as their Lord and Saviour.

It accomplishes the same purpose but done in a different way, when you share your testimony with your fellow worker, neighbour, colleague, client, patient or customer and invite them to receive the same God that put a testimony in your life. You are doing this, makes you fulfilled your apostolic function.

Looking at the scripture, one can deduce two different meaning of the word "apostle". The first refers to the twelve apostles of Jesus Christ while the second meaning refers to individuals who are sent out to be messengers, ambassadors of Christ.

In this book we will consider the second meaning; an individual who has given his or her life to Jesus and by his command been ordained as Christ ambassador or his messenger sent to his work place or market place.

In *John 15:8* "Herein is my father glorified, that ye bear much fruit, so shall ye be my disciples".

God is our Father, this is what Jesus came to remind us and He emphasized It. Jesus came to bring us closer to our Father by establishing a relationship with him.

Jesus teachings centres on pleasing God our Father in all our endeavours. Jesus said he did not come on his own, he came so that the name of God might be glorified.

The essence of our lives centres on glorifying God. In the scripture quoted above it emphasized the need for our heavenly Father to be glorified. Jesus said that one of the ways to glorify God is by bearing much fruit.

Are you bearing much fruit as to please and glorify God? Any life that does bear fruit does not glorify God.

A little look at the scripture brings out to the fore the understanding that the title of being an apostle or disciple does not come first What comes first is the function of being an apostle or disciple. It is only when you have been able to bear much fruit that you can qualify to be called an apostle or disciple: *John 18:8b* "That ye bear much fruit, so shall ye be my disciples." What qualities you to be Jesus' disciples or an apostle is only when you bear much fruit. Without bearing fruit you are not qualified to be called a disciple or an apostle.

The process of bearing fruit is not a prerogative right or function of ministers of God or pastors. Every believer is called out to bear fruit, to evangelize, to preach. In *Mark 16:15-20* "And he said unto them Go ye into all world, and preach the gospel to every creature. He that believeth and is baptized shall be damned. And these signs shall follow them that believe, in my name shall they cast out devils, they shall speak with new tongues, they shall take up serpents and if they drink any deadly thing, it shall not hurt them, they shall lay hands on the sick, and they shall recover.... And they went forth and preached everywhere, the Lord working with them and confirming the word with signs following".

It is important to note that the generic meaning of an apostle does not only refer to the twelve apostles. There are other God messengers that the bible referred to as apostles. For example, Barnabas is referred to as apostle in *Acts 13:2, Acts 14:4*, while Andronicus and Junias two names that are not commonly remembered in the bible, were referred to as apostles in *Romans 16:7*. Titus and Epahroditus were referred to as apostles in *2 Corinthians 8:23* and *Philippians 2:25* respectively. Silas and Timothy were also referred to as apostles.

In *1 Thessalonians 2:6*. What one can deduce from the above Biblical examples is that the word apostle, besides the twelve apostles of Jesus Christ, also refers to anyone who was sent.

The word "apostle" in the Greek is called Apostollos meaning *"one sent forth"* as an ambassador of the gospel. An apostle is a minister who is sent directly by God to do a special work, in a specific place, to a specific group of people.

You are sent by God to that office or business premises to minister God's love to all creatures that you come in contact with.

You don't need any specific training to share your testimonies with your colleague, customers, client or patient. You equally do not need any training to invite people to give their lives to Christ or to come to the fellowship or church.

In *John 2:28-30*: "The woman then left her water pot, and went her way into the city, and saith to the men, come, see a man, which told me all things that ever I did, is not this the Christ? Then they went out of the city, and came unto him".

The woman that met Jesus at the well was not referred as Jesus' disciples or apostles but her encounter with Jesus made her to leave her water pot at the well and ran into the city to share her testimony and invite people to see Jesus.

She went on a mission to tell people about Jesus. This qualified her to be called an apostle.

Looking at the scripture referred to in *John 18:15*: and taking cognizance of the roles of the disciples of Jesus, the woman at the well can be properly addressed as a disciples or an apostle.

The disciples of Jesus in *John 4* went into the city to look for food and not souls. They saw food and saw people but never ministered to the people they saw in the city. Their major concern was to satisfy their flesh.
The woman at the well went into the same city, saw food and people but ministered to the people and brought the people to Jesus. When the two "commodities" arrived; the food brought by the disciples and the people brought by the women, Jesus abandoned the food and ministered to the people. The disciples who were not sensitive to Jesus' mission on earth and the call of God upon their lives said, were surprise at Jesus' response concerning the food they brought.

See what Jesus answered them in *John 4:31-38*: "In the mean while his disciples prayed him, saying, master, eat. But he said unto them, I have meat to eat that ye know not of. Therefore, said the disciples one to another, Hath any man brought him ought to eat? Jesus saith unto them, my meat is to do the will of him that sent me, and to finish his work, Say not ye, there are yet four months, and then cometh harvest? Behold, I say unto you, lift up your eyes, and look on the fields, for they are white already to harvest. And he that reapeth receiveth wages, and gathereth fruit unto life eternal that both he that soweth and he that reapeth may rejoice together. And herein is that saying true, one soweth, and another reapeth. I sent you to reap that whereon ye bestowed no labour, other men labored, and ye are entered into their labours".

Judging from the incident that took place in *John 4* in line with *John 15:8* it is proper to call the woman at the well as Jesus disciple or apostle. The real followers of Jesus in that dispensation didn't merit to be called disciples or apostles.

Although Jesus was hungry, He knew that soul winning is more important to God than any other activities in the church. Jesus used that occasion to teach us that soul wining is a priority in the kingdom of God and it is a sole responsibility of anyone who had encountered Him.

The woman at the well did not receive any permission from Jesus or God. Jesus did not call her apostle Samaritan woman or disciple Samaritan woman but by her fruit, she registered her name as indeed an apostle of Jesus.

The woman did not receive or hear any call from Jesus to go into the city to invite people to give their lives to Christ.

The mission of every apostle changes once he or she encounters God. Saul became Paul by an encounter with Jesus. Paul started functioning as an apostle that encounter with the Master.

We shouldn't wait to hear a call from God before we step out of our comfort zone. The moment you encounter Jesus and align yourself with the ministry of reconciling men back to God you are qualified biblically to be referred to as an apostle.

If you share your testimony directly or through a book to invite people to give their lives to Christ like the Samarian woman at the well, you are functioning as an apostle and indeed you are an apostle. If peradventure you are active in this ministry at your place of work, business, neighbourhood market, you are indeed an apostle at the market place.

An apostle is called out by God to minister to a certain group of people. This call is not of men but for enlarging of God's kingdom.

The woman at the well we discussed earlier was called by God by her encounter with Jesus to reach the people in her city. If that woman can succeed as an apostle despite her pedigree, we can also succeed as apostle at the market place.

Some of us are doing what the disciples of Jesus did in John 4 where their focus was on food and not the souls.

Today, our primary focus in our place of work or business is to make, climb the highest position we can occupy, get the highest promotion we can get. This is achieved at the expense of our primary duty at the market place. Our personal interest has beclouded God's expectation from us in the market place. We have so much entangled ourselves in the affairs of the world that we don't have the integrity to function as an apostle at the market place.

The ministry of Jesus did not begin without his looking out for those who are already apostles in the market place.

In *Luke 4:28-29* "And all thing in the synagogue when they heard these things were filled with wrath. And rose up and thrust him out of the city, and led him into the brow of the hill whereon their city was built, that they might cast him down head long" This is an account of how Jesus message was rejected in the synagogue, his personality was rejected and his ministry was rejected in the synagogue.

At the time of Jesus first appearance, his message and ministry was to the members of the synagogue but unfortunately they were filled with wrath and thrust him out of the synagogue.

If Jesus had relied on the members of synagogue his ministry and vision would have ended.

Jesus offered the first opportunity of recruiting his disciples and apostles to the members of the synagogue but they rejected it. Jesus did not allow that to dampen his ministry, He went on to look for the apostles in the market place.

In *Luke 5 :1-3* "And it came to pass, that as the people pressed upon him to hear the word of God, he stood by the lake of Gennesaret, and saw two ships standing by the lake, but the fishermen were gone out of there, and were washing their nets. And he entered into one of the ships, which was Simon's, and prayed him that he would thrust out a little from the land. And he sat down, and taught the people out of the ship".

When Jesus departed from the synagogue in Luke 4, He continued his journey in Luke 5. The bible said that people pressed upon Him to hear the word of God. Jesus saw a mammoth crowd; he could have started a crusade or revival camp meeting but he did not.

As the people were pressing upon Jesus, He was pressing unto the market place, He was not looking for people to preach to. The people were actually following him so they could hear the word of God.

Jesus knew that His mission on earth is not only to preach the word of God but He must raise or commission men who will take over the work of the kingdom After His departure.

Jesus continued His journey until he got to the market place known as the lake of gennesaret (modern day ship yard or ports authority). When Jesus got to the water front he still did not start preaching until he had entered the office of one of the market place apostles.

At the time Jesus entered the boat of Peter, Peter was not an apostle, neither were the other fishermen at the lake. They were all fishermen doing their business at their place of work. Today, Jesus is visiting us in our places of work, business activities, known as market place.

Jesus did not look for qualified or trained apostles. It is Jesus responsibility to choose you, prepare and train you and release you into the same environment you have been living or working.

Today, the vessel Jesus is looking for is not a boat to enter but a human vessel he can enter, that is why he said in *Revelation 3:20:*

"Behold I stand at the door, and knock if any man hear my voice, and open the door, I will come into him, and will sup with him, and he with me".

Jesus did not ask Peter to preach to the people because he was still human but now He is not in human form, Jesus wants to preach to all the people around us pressing to hear the word of salvation, the wind of healing, the word of deliverance.

Are you willing to make yourself available as a vessel Jesus can use and begin to reconcile men back to God? In *1 Corinthians. 9:16-17:* "For though I preach the gospel, I have nothing to glory of, for necessity is laid upon me, yea, woe is unto me, if I preach not the gospel, for I do this thing willingly, I have a reward, but if against my will, a dispensation of the gospel is committed unto me".

Every work you do for God as an apostle in the market place is a fulfillment of God's purpose for your life.

When Jesus finished preaching in Luke 5, He performed a miracle that gave Peter an opportunity to encounter God. However, the purpose of Jesus going to the water front was not merely to preach to the crowd. He has the crowd with him before He got to the lake of Gennessaret. Jesus was on a mission!

What was this mission that spurred Jesus to proceed to the lake the lake of Gennessaret even when He had the crowd to preach to?

What will make Jesus to keep on going to the lake when the crowd he was looking for were already with him? He was not worried about losing them or some of them turning back half the journey to the lake of Gennessaret.

Jesus was not yet satisfied despite that the crowd were pressing on him to hear the word.

Jesus performed that miracle of the great catch to give Peter an opportunity to see the ability of God. **Luke 5:8** "when Simon Peter saw it, he fell down at Jesus knees, saying depart from me; for I am a sinful man, O Lord".

This is the reason Jesus went to the lake; to give men or women to encounter God through God, thereafter their purpose for living. Remember, until you encounter God through Jesus Christ the purpose for your living will never be revealed to you.

The reason you are confused moving from one issue to another is that the purpose for your living has not been revealed to you. Jesus have given us several opportunities to encounter God through him but we have allowed such opportunities to slip our fingers. We have remained were we are without meaningful progress in our lives because of sheer ignorance.

Despite the crowd, Jesus was looking for the apostles at the market place. Who then are these apostles at the market place? They are the fishermen, lawyers, doctors, nurses, pharmacist, engineers and technicians, surveyors, professionals and business persons.

When Jesus met the professional at lake of Gennessaret He informed him the purpose why he was looking for him in *Luke 5:10b*. **"And Jesus said unto Simon, fear not, from henceforth thou shalt catch men"**.

Every professional or businessman or woman who have had an encounter with God through Jesus Christ is not exempted from the above instruction Jesus gave to Simon Peter. Jesus is saying to every professional and business person, fear not, from henceforth thou shalth catch men.

The essence of this book is to show how by becoming the light of the world, you can catch men for God through Jesus Christ. The purpose of becoming the light of the world as an apostle at the market place is that the Gentiles, Unbelievers and kings shall come to your light and your rising see *Isaiah. 60:3* "And the gentiles shall come to thy light and kings to the brightness of thy rising".

In *Isaiah. 60:4a* "Lift up thine eyes roundabout and see; all they gather themselves together, they come to thee.". Everyone in the darkness including insects and animals runs to light. Light is a natural attraction to both humans and animals. So, when as a professional or businessman becomes the apostle in the market place you will automatically become the light of the world. When this happens people get attracted to you and you catch them for God.

All the people Jesus ordained as his first apostles were mostly professionals, businessmen or civil servant (tax collectors) who by proving the calling of God upon their lives were now called apostles. All they did for Jesus was recorded in Acts of Apostles and epistles.

It is important to note that most activities of Jesus' apostles recorded in the Acts of Apostles were not event that took place in the synagogue (present day church) but activities that took place at the market place.

The apostles did not become apostles for what they did in the synagogue (church) they became apostles by reason of what they did for God in work place, markets, people's home etc.

If the apostles were waiting for the religious rulers of their time to accept them and give them pulpit to preach perhaps there wouldn't have been any events recorded in their name.

It is the apostles at the market place that received Jesus and His mission. It is same apostles at the market place that Jesus used to start his ministry. The apostles at the market place where first professionals, civil servants and businessmen before they become apostles at the market place. It is their encounter with God through Jesus Christ and their willingliness to be used by God that made them to become apostles at the market place.

The apostles at the market place are referring to men who are already working as professionals, government or company workers, in their place of work, who sees an opportunity to promote God's kingdom either by preaching to people or inviting them to the fellowship or giving them Christian's tracts.

Apostles at the market place are those professionals like lawyers, doctors, pharmacist, engineers, surveyors, technicians, teachers, civil servants etc. who at the place of their work shares the love and testimonies of God to their fellow workers, colleagues, customers, clients or neighbours.

Every believer that is engaged with one business or job is qualified to be an apostle in the market place.

What qualifies believers as an apostle at the market place is when they engage in the kingdom of God's work while working in their offices or places of business.

So as a professional businessperson, civil or public servant God expect you to be an apostle at the market place. Will you fail God?

CHAPTER TWO

ACTIVITES IN THE MARKETPLACE

This chapter will be divided in two sections. First section will be dealing with where is the market place and the second will be dealing with what are they doing in the market place.

Where is the market place?
I may not dwell much on this because I defined and explained a market place in my book "MARKET PLACE EVANGELISM (OUTREACH) KEY TO BILLION SOULS".

But for the purpose of emphasis and for those who have not read my first book on market place evangelism, I will go on to explain the market place.

The market place within this context refers to a place of economic, political, educational or social activities outside the church.

A market place is any environment that brings two or more persons to engage in one activity or function. The market place within this context does not refer only to where economic profit is derived.

Where is the market place? The market place we have seen comprises the following but not limited to them.

a. **GOVERNMENT:** Activities that goes on in this section is higher than any other sector in the world. It has the highest number of human activities because of the attraction and benefit of power associated with it. This sector is where people spent a lot of money to acquire or even kill in order to get the power and influence associated with it.

When we talk about government we are referring to the executive, legislative and judicial arm of the government.

All these platforms provide an opportunities for daily human activities and human participation. Take for example the executive arm of government comprising the president and his vice, his aides, personal assistant and all ministers. The ministers also have personal assistant, personal advisers with many staff working under them.

The executive arm, continues with the governors, and their deputies their aides, personal advisers, commissioners, directors and workers working under them.

The executive arm also involves the local government chairman, their aides, personal assistants and workers under them.

This government positions are also associated with governmental agencies wherein appointments into various positions in the agencies are determined by those in executive positions.

There are also the contractors, suppliers of various goods and projects that comes under the human supervision of the executive. All these stated above is part of the market place.

The avenue of the market place have been avoided by true believers and some of us who found ourselves there easily lose touch with the purpose why we are there. Mordecai told Esther in ***Esther 4:13-14*** "Then Mordecai commanded to answer Esther, think not with thyself that thou shalt escape in the king's house more than all the Jews. For if thou altogether holdest thy peace at this time, ***then shall there enlargement and deliverance arise to the Jews from another place***, but thou and thy father's shall be destroyed, and ***who knoweth whether thou art come to the kingdom for such a time as this?***

Government is a market place where lives are meant to be delivered by those who understand why they are there. That is why Joseph answered thus to his brethren in **Genesis 50:20** "But as for you, ye thought evil against me; but God meant it into good to bring to pass, as it is this day, ***to save much people alive.***

Men like Nehemiah understand that government is a platform for any apostle of the market place to save lives and bring the glory of God to bear in a city and the lives of people see ***Nehemiah 2:3-5*** "And said unto the king, let the king live forever, why should not my countenance be sad, when the city, the place of my father's sepulchers, lieth waste, and the gate thereof are consumed with fire? Then the king said unto me, for what dost thou make request? So I prayed to the God of heaven. And I said unto the king, if it please the king, and if thy servant have found favour in thy sight, that thou wouldest send me into Judah, unto the city of my father's sepulchers, that I may build it".

The influence that comes from the activities in governmental sector is very powerful that it permeates other part of the market place like economy, educational system etc.

If God brings you into governmental sector and you leverage on that to preach or minister the love of God to people around you, the result will be very effective.

I remember a church that existed in Port Harcourt Rivers State of Nigeria, the then governor of the state was attending this church. This church received very high patronage because people believed that by attending the church they can be close to governor and perhaps receive some favour from the government. I cannot exhaust the function of a governmental platform in the market place, as a major platform for the existence of a market place where we can easily reach a lot of people with gospel of our Lord Jesus Christ.

b. **Educational Institutions:**

Educational institutions is another major platform for the existence of a market place.

When we talk about educational institutions our reference includes the universities, the polytechnics, college of education, vocational institutions, secondary schools (both private and public), primary and nursery schools. These is another marketplace that have constant human activities with millions of people being involved. It will be recalled that some churches today started from these institutions. The bedrock of the foundational members of these churches were people found in these educational institution.

Today, many churches have Christian fellowship in various university campus as a ground to recruit new members.

Some fellowship like Scripture Union of Nigeria have not left ministering to these platform of the market place. There are a lot of people today that are born again through the ministry of the Scripture Union while they were either in secondary school or university.

Our failure to use this platform of the market place to minister the love of God through Jesus Christ to these young ones in the universities and other educational institutions gave rise to the emergency of cultism in various universities.

Our country has suffered loss of bright students to the deadly activities of cultism in the higher institutions.

Nature abhors vacuum, when we fail to use the platform of the market place called the educational institution, the devil sees it as an opportunity to truncate the career of our future generation.

The earlier we repent from our laxity over ministering to the future generation in the educational institution the better, it is for us to save our future generation from a moral decadence and juvenile delinquency.

The important of this platform of the market place cannot be over emphasized. Any nation that plays with this platform pays dearly for it. Today most developed countries of the world are suffering from terrible violence, marriage divorce and degradation, armed robbery, etc, because of their failure to minister the love of God to the group of people found in the educational institution.

The only way any of these nations of the world that have mortgaged the future of their young generation to recover them back is to engage the ministry of the market place. Many of these young ones do not attend churches. They see church as old fashion meant only for the old folks. Today some church buildings in the developed world have been sold and now used for cinemas and hotels.

Do we want our nation to come to these? The only way to avert these future crisis of generation of vipers is to start today to minister the love of God through Jesus Christ to our generation through the market place using all available opportunities to preach the word of God to them.

Educational institutions are viable market place platform that can be effectively utilized to preach the gospel of our Lord Jesus Christ both to the old and young ones.

The educational institution comprises both the old and younger generation of any society. Once we get it right at this market place you can be sure that the future is bright.

The future of every nation has a lot to do with activities that goes on in this market place, neglect it doom is waiting, exploit it for God boom will surely come.

c.   **PRISON:**

This is a special platform of a market place. It is a platform that is open to everybody. As many people you found there are there either as workers employed by government or those that contravened the laws of the land and the government sent them there for punishment.

Admittance into this sector is restricted to those who are employed to work there as prison wardens or those that did not apply to work but were taken there by law enforcement process. Whichever way a person find himself it does not deprive you the opportunity to receive the love of God through Jesus Christ.

This is not a platform many people have received calling from God to go and minister, they by circumstances, have come there and faithfully became an instrument in the hand of God to minister both to the prisoners and prison warden.

In *Acts 16:25, 31:32* "And at midnight Paul and Silas prayed, and sang praise unto God and the prisoners heard them… And they said, believe on the Lord Jesus Christ, and thou shalt be saved, and thy house. And they spake unto him the word of the Lord, and to all that were in his house".

Joseph in the bible did not plan to be in the prison but circumstances beyond his control brought him to the prison. *Gen 40:3* "And he put them in ward in the house of the captain of the guard, into the prison, the place where Joseph was bound".

Gen. 39:20-21 "And Joseph's master took him, and put him into the prison, a place where the kings' prisoners were bound and he was there in the prison. But the Lord was with Joseph, and showed him mercy, and gave him favour in the sight of the keeper of the prison".

Joseph took his fate as he found it but did not loose his fellowship with God because he was in prison. He recognized that he was an apostle in the market place, circumstances around him should not make him lose sight of who he was and he did not lose his fellowship with God. The bible said that the Lord was with Joseph even in that prison.

Are you in a prison of life where circumstances have made you to start losing focus of who you are, please don't forget that you are an apostle at the market place, creation is waiting for your manifestation.

You do not need to be in prison before you develop an interest to minister to those who work in prison or who are prisoners. Understand that prison is another platform for market place activities. Testimonies abound of people who received Christ while they were in prison and as a result of their giving their lives to Christ received amnesty and set free from the prison.

Some months ago my wife took some women in our zone of the Full Gospel Businessmen Fellowship to Port Harcourt Prison, where they organized prison outreach for the prisoners. At the end of the day, some of the prisoners gave their lives to Christ while some rededicated their lives back to God.

d.   **ECONOMY**

Economy activities are in different dimensions but for the purpose of this chapter I will limit our discourse on the economy activities that goes on in the banks, insurance, telecommunication, oil industry, ports authority etc.

These section is a section where a lot of people are engaged as employees or agents or contractors or suppliers.

Economic activities have great attraction to those aspiring to work after graduation or change jobs or those aspiring to be rich as investor. Whatever affects this sector in a nation affects every facets of activities of the nation.

Sometimes governmental activities are reduced or cut down as a result of low activities in this section. It is a section that attracts the young graduates, it attracts investors, it attract workers looking for greener pastures.

Union or associations have been formed as result of these economic activities. There is no nation in the world today that do not have banks, insurance companies, telecommunication, port authority or airport, and number of people employed or engaged in these areas are quite enormous that their number run in millions.

Everyone you meet in this section is there for what he/she wants to profit or receive as wages or rewards. But often people involved in these economic activities have streamlined their activities to centre only on the profit that they want to make.

Today the number of banks in existences with their branches are numerous. The insurance companies are many with branches all over the nation, sea ports and airport are places of beehives of human activities.

All those we come in contact with in these economic sectors are candidates of God's love. We have a responsibility as we come in contact with them to share the love of God through Jesus Christ.

It is an attraction that cannot be over emphasized. It has daily activities that we cannot exhaust easily. The economic activities in the market place are very big platform for us to minister effectively as apostles in the market place.

e. **HOMES**

Many have not realized that several homes are qualified to be referred to as a market place. It was in the house that Andrew ministered to Peter and told him that he has seen the Messiah, he should come and see him.

When Jesus was ministering to Zachaus he emphasized this point and told Zachaeus that salvation has come to his house in ***Luke 19:9*** "And Jesus said unto him, this day is salvation come to this house, for so much as he also a son of Abraham".

As long as you are a son of Abraham your house can be a market place where you can function effectively as an apostle of the market place. Those in your house can be ministered to or visitors that come to your house can receive salvation in your house. You can as well minister salvation to people you meet in other people's houses.

I remember some years back when I was involved in family deliverance, this took me to several cities and villages in my country with my group; part of what we did when we come to any family to carry out family deliverance is to minister the gift of salvation to them first before starting the family deliverance. I discovered that it was an effective way of ministering salvation to those who wants their families to be delivered from one bondage to the other.

When Joseph was brought into Potiphar's house, he did not see himself only as a house help but he saw himself as an apostle in the market place.

The realization of whom he was regulated his activities in the house which attracted God's favour to that househood. ***Gen. 39:2-4*** "And the Lord was with Joseph, and he was a prosperous man, and he was in the house of his master the Egyptian. And his master saw that the Lord was with him, and that the Lord made all that he did to prosper in his hand. And Joseph found grace in his sight and he served him, and he made him overseer over his house, and all that he had, he put into his hand".

The miracle that Naaman received in his house was by the act of a house help who saw herself as an apostle in the market place and she had a God that can perform a miracle in ***2 Kings 5:2-3*** "And the Syrians had gone out by companies, and had brought away captive out of the land of Israel a little maid, and she waited on Naaman's wife. And she said unto her mistress, would God my Lord were with the prophet that is in Samaria! For he would recover him of his leprosy". The girl, though she was a house help and a captive, did not allow her circumstances and position stop her from introducing her God to the master.

How many of us today working under a Muslim or occultic master will have the boldness to introduce God to her master? Naaman's maid must have conducted herself in a way first that her mistress will believe and trust her judgment. She must have behaved in a way that the master, knowing that the suggestion is coming from the maid, will listen and carry out the instruction. She is indeed an example of an apostle in the market place who saw an opportunity to introduce the love of God and the healing power of God to Naaman. I don't need a prophet to tell me that Naaman recognized God after that healing encounter.

I don't need to be informed that heaven recorded it for the maid, although the Bible did not write her name. If the Bible will include and record her activity in her master's home, it is sure that heaven must have recognized that she fulfilled her mission here on earth.

It is important to know that it was not only Naaman that went to see the prophet. Naaman as captain of the army must have gone with his entourage. Those who accompanied Naaman also had opportunity to hear and see the love and healing power of God.

So the maid not only caught Naaman for God but caught all those that follow Naaman. Remember that the king of Syria gave Naaman permission to go to Israel *2 Kings 5:5* "And the King of Syria said go to, go, and I will send a letter unto the king of Israel. And he departed, and took with him ten talents of silver, and six thousand pieces of gold and ten changes of raiment".

From the foregoing the king and his cabinet also heard and saw the love and healing power of God. God had used the maid to minister to Naaman's wife directly and indirectly to Naaman, his servants the king of Syria and his cabinets.

The chains of people in Syria who heard about God through the simple act of an apostle in the market place is quite enormous that cannot be fully enumerated.

The maid did not see herself only as a captive, she did not see herself as a maid but she saw herself also as God's ambassador, an apostle in the market place, who must use every available opportunity to introduce God effectively to those around her.

If the maid can do it in a strange land, why can't you do it where you are now. God is watching you and waiting to receive your bountiful harvest of souls.

f. BUSINESS CENTRE

The world today is internet propelled society where today you can buy online and it will be brought to your house.

Internet is the highest network of market place. Before believers will understand the purpose of internet and cable television, the unbelievers have gone ahead to dominate and project their master with so many pornographic pictures and others.

In the world of internet, you can read books called E-books, you can read newspapers, access any information you desire from the internet.

Internet is the largest market in the market place. Every information you need about a nation, most prominent individuals, governments, schools, hotels, flights etc are all in the internet.

With internet you can reach a billion souls in less than 24 hours. You can send messages to millions of people within days.

Every product sent into the internet can be accessed by millions of people. Salvation is a product every individual needs in the world it is for both those who understand its importance and those who do not understand it.

The unfortunate issue about the package and benefits of salvation can never be understood except you receive the gift of salvation from God through Jesus Christ.

The patronage of Cybercafé's for the use internet facilities cannot be over emphasized. Even those who do not patronize Cybercafé's have many electronic devices that they can access internet facilities for example Ipad, laptop and smartphones.

I recently watched a christen movie tagged "God is not dead", towards the end of the movie everyone in a theater were asked to send to 10 persons a message that God is not dead. Imagine a crowd of 10,000 or more sending to 10 different persons such message, they would have reached 100,000 persons with the message "God is not dead".

We can copy this for those of us who have smart devices, we may be above 100 million Christians all over the world. If once every week we send a message of salvation from the word of God to at least 20 persons we know that are not believers or not strong in faith, in a year we could have reached so many millions of people for God.

So the laptop, the ipad, and countless smart devices are platform for effective market place evangelism. As apostles in the market place we can turn our ipad, iphone, handsets laptop into instrument of evangelism in the market place.

Where is the market place? The internet indeed have shown to us that we are carriers of market place if we can utilize it effectively for God.

You can effectively be an apostle in the market place if you can turn your computers, laptops, ipad/phones and smart devices into instrument of evangelism by texting Godly words to people or sending mail to them.

You may wonder if by texting the word of God or sending it by mail will produce the described result. My answer is yes! ***Hebrew. 4:12*** "For the word of God is quick and powerful and sharper than any two edged sword, piercing even to the dividing asunder of soul and spirit and of the joints and marrow and is a discerner of the thoughts and intents of the heart".

Our purpose is to reach to the soul and spirit of any man or woman who has not given his or her life to Jesus. It is only the power in the word of God that can reach out to any person.

It is the word of God that brings a conviction of the heart, our job starts by sending or preaching the word of God to somebody and it is the work of the Holy Spirit to bring a conviction in the heart of a person. ***John 6:63*** "It is the spirit that quickeneth, the flesh profiteth nothing. The words that I speak unto you, they are spirit and they are life".

g. HOSPITALS/CLINICS

Those are important platform of the market place. they play a very important role in the life of every one that comes into the world.

Most often it stands as the gate or entrance everyone comes into the world and sometimes it is also the exit gate for most of the people.

People come into the world through the hospitals/clinics and when their time for departure comes sometimes it is through hospitals/clinics that becomes the exit gate into eternity.

It is an important market place that plays one important role in the lives of everybody which we must recognize and utilize.

Pharaoh the king of Egypt also knew this important role hospitals/clinics plays in the lives of people that he decided to wait for all male Israelites children at this gate to stop them from entering into the world in Exodus 1:15-16 "And the king of Egypt spake to the Hebrew midwives of which the name of the one was Shiphrah, and the name of the other Puah, and he said, when ye do the office of a midwife to the Hebrew women, and see them upon the stools, if it be a daughter, then she shall live".

It is important to note that hospitals/clinics are a great avenue of function in the market place. Are you looking for a market place to operate, know that hospitals and clinics are a wonderful place to do that.

Every man or woman in a hospital is afraid that death could come calling so if you share the love of God and his healing power to them they will be willing to give their lives to Jesus because they need help and from wherever they help might come will be received.

It is believed that spirit of death operate more actively in the hospitals/clinics than in the homes of people. Anybody that becomes sick is taken to hospital for medical attention sometimes with prayer alert following it requesting for healing so because of issues involved at the hospitals men and women are always willing to accept Jesus in order to receive healing and stop the spirit of death against their lives.

Every doctor, pharmacist nurses or lab technicians who is a believer is a potential apostle at the market place. They occupy an important function in the life of every individual they come in contact with. And God had placed them in a position of influence to give the sick life through our Lord Jesus Christ.

The midwives referred to in Exodus 1:17-16 realized they occupy an important position of giving life or death to person and refused to heed to the instruction of the kings as recorded in Exodus 1:17 "But the midwives feared God, and did not as the king of Egypt commanded them, but saved the male children alive".

Today we can look at the midwives and said because they feared God and refused to heed to instruction of the devil through the king, they can be described as apostles in the market place. It was not their position that made them to be apostles, but it was there functions in the place of their work that earned them to be described as apostles in the market place.

The midwives saw themselves as instrument in the hand of God to give life to people or to a generation. One begin to wonder what would have happened if the midwives did not fear God and carried out the instruction of the king. What would have become the destiny of Moses? And what would have become the agenda of God as regarding the deliverance of the Israelites in Egypt declared by God about 400 years earlier.

What would have happened to the publication of bible vis a vis books of Moses in the bible like Genesis, Exodus, Leviticus and Deuteronomy and some passages in Palms. Would the ten commandments given to mankind.

There are so many questions that would have arisen. God's purpose for mankind and the nation of Israel would have been truncated.

Do you think God would have used Aaron if Moses had died in the hands of the Midwives, or would God have used Miriam considering the feebleness of Aaron and Miriam.

Sometimes you may not know the generational effect of one action you may or may not have taken for God. We understand the effect of what the Egyptian midwives did because we are conversant with the after effect of their action. Assuming they did not play their part as apostles in the market place we may not have realized the consequences of their failure if they had followed the part of omission to do what God had destined that they should do.

It is still the same thing with us in this generation. Failure to work for God in the place of your work must have led to the death of a person, a family, a nation or a generation, or may have delayed or denied the blessings an individual, family, nation or a generation might have received.

The Egyptian midwives were not Israelites, they do not serve the God of the Hebrew women, they would have been justified if they refused to listen to God and listen to their king.

If the Egyptian midwives who were not believers will fear our God and do his bidding, we who are referred to as believers have no excuse to give why we are not saving lives at the place of our works or business.

It cannot be justified with any excuse why we are not ministering to people around us who need life. We cannot be excused when we fail to give life or the bread of life to people around us that needs it. There are people the devil had condemned to death like the Egyptian king but God is expecting us to use our position in the office or business premises to deliver such one and give life to the person.

Can God count on you at the place of your work or business to give life to as many that needs it or condemned by the devil. God is waiting for you.

h. **COMPANIES/FACTORY**

Many workforce today are found in companies and factories all over the world.

There are several manufacturing companies all over the world producing different products for the entire world and most of these factories or companies employs hundreds of thousands of people as workforce.

Some of these companies or factories their workforce are more in numbers than some churches congregation.

If God places you in a position of authority in these companies or factories know that God had made you pastors of the workforce known as apostle in the market place. Companies and factories are a wonderful platform for apostles in the market place to function effectively.

Every position you occupy in such an establishment or factories is relevant to God to do what he has asked you to do in the bible to give life to those around you.

In Matt. 25:14-15 "For the kingdom of heaven is as a man travelling into a far country, who called his own servants, and delivered unto them his goods. And unto one he gave five talents, to another two, and to another one, to every man according to his several ability, and straightway took his journey".

From the above passage it is clear that God had given to each and every one of us the talent that suit our ability, it is left with us to trade with the talent God had deposited in us for him.

God is not looking at the position you occupy whether as a manager, supervisor or ordinary employee of the company, what God is looking at what you can make out of the talent He has given to you.

In Matt. 25:16-17 "Then he that had received the five talents went and traded with the same, and made them other five talents. And likewise he that had received two, he also gained other two".

It is important to say that God is looking at what you make out of the position He gave you. Are you using it to promote His kingdom, are you using it to give life to people through Jesus Christ. What you do with your talent is very important to God and that determines the reward you receive from God.

In Matt. 25:20-21 "And so he that had received five talents came and brought other five talents, saying Lord thou deliverest unto me five talents behold, I have gained beside them five talents more. His Lord said unto him, well done, thou good and faithful servant, thou has been faithful over a few things, I will make thee ruler over many things, enter thou into the joy of the Lord" what God answered the man He gave five talents that traded it and got another five talents, is the same answer He gave to the man He gave two talents.

Matt. 25:22-23 "He also that had received two talents came and said, Lord thou deliverest unto me two talents; behold, I have gained two other talents beside them. His Lord said unto him, well done, good and faithful servant, thou has been faithful over a few things, I will make thee ruler over many things enter thou into the joy of thy Lord".

As it is then so it is today there are people who are really functioning with the talents God have given to them irrespective of the quantity or the position. They are also been rewarded at the place of their work. They are the apostles in the market place in the place of their work.

Today there are some people who are still behaving like the man with one talent.

They see themselves as members of the congregation. They said to themselves that they are not pastors or Sunday school teachers, it is not their function to preach or minister to someone. The only role God has given them to sit in the pew every Sunday or during mid week service and give their tithe or offering.

They are to be likened to the man who took his one talent and hid it Matt. 25 24-25 "Then he which had received the one talent came and say Lord, I knew thee that thou art an hard man, reaping where thou hast not sown, and gathering, where thou hast not strained. And I was afraid and went and hid thy talent in the earth, Lo, there thou hast that is thine".

Are you among those who have refused to give life or preach to someone at the place of your work or business, you can be likened to that fellow that went and hid his talent.

You are in a position to minister the love of God to your fellow workers and you are hiding your identity, you don't want them to know your identity.

You may be among those who believe that it is only in the church that you should preach and souls are dying and going to hell fire and you are comfortable at your comfort zone.

Have you not recognized yourself as an apostle in the market place. Have you refused to accept that you are an apostle in the market place for fear of preaching to someone at your place of work.

Let heaven not see you as been among those that are hiding their talent because the same judgment God passed on to the man who hid his talent may be the portion of a man who ought to be an apostle in the market place but refused to function as one.

Matt. 25:26, 30 "His Lord answered and said unto him, thou wicked and slothful servant, thou knewest that I reap where I sowed not, and gather where I have not strained ….. And cast ye that unprofitable servant into darkness, there shall be weeping and gnashing of teeth". God is the one that gave you that job and placed you in that position in the company or factory so that you can be his apostle in the market place.

Are you doing that now if no it is not late you can start today, that is the essence of this book not to condemn you but to encourage and open your eyes to issues you have neglected or do not understand.

God is waiting for you to respond to his call at the market place. God has always use a worker to be his apostle either in the full time ministry or in the market place.

The most important thing to God is to carry out your responsibility to the satisfaction of God.

God is interested in using workers to do his work for him see 1 Kings 19:19 "So he departed thence, and found Elisha the son of Shaphat, who was plowing with twelve yoke of oxen before him, and he with the twelfth, and Elijah passed by him, and cast his mantle upon him".

i. **MARKET /SHOPPING MALL**

The market is divided into two sections. The traditional market and the modern market known as shopping malls, stores etc.

All these provide a platform for market place evangelism if it is properly harnessed. Anybody can feature effectively as an apostle in the market place.

Some months ago I have an arrangement with a pastor who on weekly basis moves from one store to another store on one to one personal evangelism. The result has been quite tremendous.

This is a platform that does not require any qualification to be enrolled you can move into any market in the world or any shopping mall to carry out any evangelistic activities. Remember that there is no home in the world that does not have something to do with this platform, weekly a member of a family or their personal representative must go to the market or shopping mall to buy household items for the family use.

We can through this platform minister to someone who will become a carrier of God's message to the entire family. Any person who received life through Jesus Christ will definitely share it with his family members or become a prayer warrior for the family members to receive the mercy and love of God.

It is important to remember that daily activities occur at both traditional market and shopping mall. It is needful we exploit this opportunity to the benefit of God's kingdom and to His glory.

Recently the terrorist in Nigeria carried out a suicide bomber attack at a shopping mall in Abuja and a traditional market in Borno State of Nigeria.

Why did they target the traditional market and the shopping mall, because they realized that it is an avenue to achieve greater result of souls destroyed?

We the believers can be the apostles in the market place God is looking for to invade the traditional market and shopping mall with our megaphones, voice magazines, Christian tracts, bibles and Christian literatures to give life to souls in the market. The terrorist goes there to give them death, we the believers as apostles in the market place can give life to people in the market or shopping mall.

This platform is one of the greatest avenues for market place evangelism where you can reach the rich and poor of the society. It is also the one that you do not require any statutory permission to enter in order to do your apostolic function as apostle in the market place.

All that you need is courage as God advised Joshua in the book of Josh. 1:7 "Only be thou strong and very courageous that thou mayest observe to do according to all the law, which Moses my servant commanded thee, turn not from it to the right hand or to the left that thou mayest prosper withersoever thou goest".

The market place also include trade fairs, trade exhibition, book exhibition and others. This we have found to be a very wonderful avenue to minister life to unbelievers.

I belonged to the market place outreach (MPO) of the Full Gospel Business Men Fellowship International Nigeria. In South South 1 Region we have been carrying out market place outreaches at the Port Harcourt Trade Fair for the past 4 years, above 800 persons have given their lives to God through Jesus Christ.

This should be an eye opener to all apostles in the market place as a trade fairs, food exhibition, book fair are been carried out in the cities we live we should see it as an opportunity to organize outreaches to minister the love and mercy of God to people that attends such fairs.

Remember that traditional market and shopping malls are highly patronized by people of different race and religious background we can use that platform to function as an apostle in the market place.

You don't need to have a store or a shop in a market place or shopping mall before you function as an apostle in the said market or shopping mall.

It is open to as many that will utilize the opportunity to minister life to people. A lot of people in these markets or shopping mall desire their business to progress, you can go there in the name of praying for their business or their marriage minister to their soul as well as pray for their business.

j. Neighbourhood / office

These are another platform for an apostle of the market place. There is a member of the Full Gospel Business Men Fellowship International Nigeria who became a member because in the company she was working, there was a colleague who lived in her neighbourhood that carries her to work every day. That man severally invited her to the fellowship of the Full Gospel Business Men Fellowship after several declines she accepted to attend the fellowship as a mark of respect to the colleague.

On this fateful day she attended the fellowship meeting with her husband and on that day both of them gave their lives to Jesus and today God had used this sister to minister to several souls and she is still ministering.

That brother that invited this sister to the fellowship meeting cannot quantify what God had used the said person he invited to the fellowship to do and is still doing in her life. She does not only have life and the blessings of God but she has become an apostle in the market place ministering life to people and has become a blessing to the body of Christ and her generation.

In my other book I published I shared about a man who came to the fellowship meeting of the Full Gospel Business Men Fellowship International where I ministered in Yenagoa Bayelsa State of Nigeria, the man was invited by his neighbor and gave his life to Jesus and after few days he gave his life to Christ, he died.

It is on record that the neighour has helped him to receive life before his journey into eternity.

Office environment is a normal platform for every apostle in the market place to operate. Office is the first market place God had given to you as a place for you to function effectively as an apostle in the market place.

Your neighourhood is also another important and easy platform for you to function as an apostle in the market place. Your office or work place and neighourhood is a market place where any person can function as an apostle in the market place.

k. OTHERS

Space and time will not permit me to itemize and give a detailed explanation of the places to be considered as market place.

It is important for us to know some of these platform for market place so that you can recognize the opportunities it offered to you whenever you see it. Few I can mention here are as follows:

i. TRANSPORTATION

This is a market place platform that enables us the privilege to minister to somebody we may not have met before and may not meet the person again in life. Transportation as a platform draws an example from Acts 8:26 – 30 "And the angel of the Lord spake unto Philip, saying, arise and go forward the south unto the way that goeth down from Jerusalem unto Gaza, which is desert. And he arose and went and behold, a man of Ethiopia, an eunuch of great authority under Candace queen of the Ethiopians who had the charge of all her treasure and had come to Jerusalem for worship was returning and sitting in his chariot read Esuias the prophet. Then the spirit said unto Philip, go near and join thyself to this chariot."

The obedience of Philip to the commandment of God led Philip ministering to the Ethiopian Eunuch. This goes to emphasis to us that those fellow passengers with us in the bus, car, train, plane, ship and any other means of transportation are people God had positioned around us to receive the love and mercy of God through us. Don't miss such opportunity any other time it comes to you.

ii OFFICE

Different office are designed by God to be used by the apostles of the market place to minister his love and mercy to those in need of it.

Our law offices are platforms for market place activities for lawyers. By virtue of the nature of their work they see many people, a new face virtually every day, this becomes a platform to share the word of God and minister salvation to them.

Another professional that can turn his office to market place activity is the medical doctor. Their opportunity to share the word of God and minister to their patient cannot be over emphasized. Everybody who comes to a doctor desires to live more than any other person. Sometimes they are beclouded with the fear of imminent death. It is true nobody wants to die.

In that state of that patient a doctor that sees himself as an apostle with a mission can utilize the opportunity to present the real life that comes from Jesus to the person.

Accounting office, surveyors office, architects office, engineering firm and many more are wonderful platform for any of us having this offices to minister the love and mercy of God to our clients or visitors.

iii. Bus stop/ train station

This is another platform for market place activity the number of people that comes to the bus stop to board a taxi or bus to respective places can outnumber a church with an average attendance.

We should utilize the opportunity bus stop of various cities offers to us especially in the wee hours of the day both in the morning and the evening.

Train station is also another busy area for areas where the train is functioning effectively.

I remember in 2012 during the Paralympics events in London, my children, I and one of our friends in London, went to a train station near the event and started sharing Christian tracts and FGB voice magazines.

We can invade those train stations or airport departure hall with voice magazines of the Full Gospel Business Men Fellowship International or any other good Christian tracts as a way of ministering to people.

iv.   **PARKS AND GARDEN**

This can also be an avenue to operate our market place activity. In 2013, I and my family went to London for another summer holiday, one of the days we were in London my son Praise Divine Victory told us that God asked him to share Christian tracts. We made available some Christian tracts and took him and his sisters to a park close to where we were lodging and my son started sharing christen tracts to all the adults we met at the park. They all collected the tracts from him and it is our believe that the tracts will minister to them.

Events at the stadium have moved some men to go there and share the love and mercy of God to spectators. So we can go to the stadium with a mission to share Christian literatures or minister to the people there.

The most important thing to understand about the market place is that it is anywhere souls of men can be found. It does not matter what name is given to the place, events like child dedication, marriage anniversary, opening of new house, birthday parties, graduation and thanksgiving can be utilized by the celebrant as an opportunity to minister to people with message of salvation.

The most important commodity in the market place is souls of men. The trading commodity in the market place is souls of people. John 3:16 "For God so love the world that he gave his only begotten son, that whosoever believeth in him should not perish, not have everlasting life".

Remember 2 Peter 3:9b "Not willing that any should perish, but that all should come to repentance" .

God does not want anyone to perish that is the reason why he sent his only begotten son to come and die for our sins, so that all of us should receive eternal life.

Since God do not want anybody to perish, I don't think we want people to perish because of our failure to do our part.

It is our great responsibility to execute and bring to pass in the life of our neighours, colleagues, friends and family members what Jesus did on the cross of Calvary.

WHAT ARE THEY DOING IN THE MARKET PLACE

The apostles in the market place did not enter the market place as pastors or ministers of God.

They did not enter the market place with intention to preach the gospel but as they continue their normal professional duties they discover that outside their professional work there is an inert desire to fulfill a calling or to fill up an emptiness in the heart of others.'

Most apostles in market place started as professionals or business men and women or normal civil or public servant but as Jesus spoke to Simon Peter in Luke 5:10b " And Jesus said unto Simon, fear not, from henceforth shalt catch men" so God had spoken to some of us or is still speaking to us.

Luke the writer of the gospel according to Luke and the Acts of Apostles was a medical doctor, who was commissioned by the authority to investigate and write his report of the Christian organization. In Luke 1:1-4 "For as much as many have taken in hand to set forth in order a declaration of those things which are most surely believed among us, which from the beginning were eye witnesses and ministers of the world, it seemed good to me also having had perfect understanding of all things from the very first, to write unto thee in order, most excellent Theophilus, that thou mightiest know the certainly of those things, wherein thou has been instructed"

Also in Acts 1:1 "The former treatise have I made, O Theophilus of all that Jesus began both to do and teach".

Luke was not among the apostles Jesus called, he was also not among the apostles the twelve apostles nominated, he also did not receive his apostleship the way Paul received his.

He started as a medical doctor, then a writer of events, commissioned to do his ordinary duty to a constituted authority but ended up writing two of the largest gospel in the new testament. Do we need a prophet to tell us that Luke fulfilled his calling in his market place and thereby ended up fulfilling a divine agenda.
Generation upon generation have read his two books in the new testament, more people will still read the two books and draw spiritual inspiration from them.

If Luke was not in the market place to fulfill a divine agenda, the Holy Spirit act in the lives of the apostles of Jesus and Paul would have been lost without a record for the future generation. God is indeed a wonderful and perfect master.

Peter did not start his life as an apostle, he was not found in the synagogue when Jesus visited the synagogue in Luke 4, but Jesus found Peter in Luke 5 at the seaside. What was Peter doing, he was simply doing his professional job as a fisherman.

In Luke 5:1-3 "And it came to pass that as the people pressed upon him to hear the word of God, he stood by the lake of Gennesaret, and saw two ships standing by the lake, but the fishermen were gone out of the them, and were washing their nets. And he entered into one of the ships which was Simon's, and prayed him that he would thrust out a little from the land. and he sat down, and taught the people out of the ship".

This goes to confirm that Peter was just a fisherman who had really a bad season. But if Jesus had waited for Peter at the synagogue perhaps he would not have seen Peter and he would have ended his life as unfulfilled fisherman.

At the time Jesus arrived the scene Peter was not preaching to anybody, he was not hearing any testimony because he had none to share. Peter was washing his nets like others which is part of the routine of a fisherman.

Peter had toiled all night what was Peter toiling for, it is not any other thing than fish or his business. Just as it is today we are toiling for one thing or the other. Luke 5:5 "And Simon answered said unto him, master, we have toiled all the night, and have taken nothing nevertheless at thy word I will let down the net".

Stop toiling for anything, Jesus said in Matt. 11:28 "Come unto me, all ye that labour and are heavy laden, and I will give you rest".
Did Peter receive rest or not? My answer is yes but that rest only came when Peter responded to the call of Jesus at his own (Peter) market place. See Luke 5:10b "And Jesus said unto Simon, fear not, from henceforth thou shalt catch men".

See Peter's response to Jesus demand in Luke 5:11 "And when they had brought their ships to land, they forsook all and followed him".

From the above scripture it is clear that it was not only Peter that responded to the call of God in the market place.

The scripture said that when they had brought their ships to land, they forsook all and followed him. Remember that those that followed Peter to forsook all and follow Jesus included Andrew, James and John the sons of Zebedee.

Even if your encounter with Jesus is not like Simon Peter, you as a believer can join people like James and John to follow Jesus and become an apostle in the market place. James and John did not wait until Jesus enter their boat before they took a decision to follow him. They only saw what Jesus did in the life of Simon Peter and believe that if they follow Jesus that which Jesus did in the life of Peter, He will equally do same unto them. I agree with the opinion of James and John because God is not a respecter of any person as in Acts 10:34, 35 "Then Peter opened his mouth, and said of a truth I perceive that God is no respecter of persons; but in every nation he that feareth him, and worketh righteousness, is accepted with him.

Don't wait until you receive call like Paul or Jesus enters your boat as long as you are a believer you are called to function effectively in the market place.

Not only did James and John became among the three closest apostles of Jesus, their books became part of the gospel written in the bible. Inspiration from their books today have affected positively so many Christians in the past and the present.

Paul's entrance into the market place as an apostle is quite dramatic. From been a persecutor of the Christian faith to a propagator of the sane christian faith. Paul was a trained lawyer and a practitioner of Mosaic law (Judaism), known as the law of Moses.

Paul became obsessed with his desire to ensure the enforcement of the law of Moses perhaps as a constitutional lawyer of his time.

Having being brought up under Jewish scholars, he combined his righteous knowledge with his constitutional knowledge to attack those whom he alleged that must have contravened the laws of God and the laws of the Jews.

Paul embarked on a journey of destruction of Christians, but ended that journey as a chosen apostle in the market place.

In Acts 9:1-2 "And Saul, yet breathing out threatening and slaughter against the disciples of the Lord, went unto the high priest. And desired of him letters to Damascus to the synagogues, that if he found any of this way, whether they were men or woman, he might bring them bound unto Jerusalem?.

In Acts 9:5 "And he said who are thou Lord? And the Lord said, I am Jesus whom thou persecutest: it is hard for thee to kick against the pricks".

If Paul despite his persecution of the church still have a chance to become an apostle in the market place, you equally have such opportunity. Are you ready to surrender as Paul did. Know that it is hard for you to kick against the pricks.

How long will you fight against invitation for you in the market place, you prefer to toil all night rather than respond to the simple call of God to make your life better. God is still waiting. The chance and opportunity God kept for you is still there. It is good you grab this opportunity before it is late as described in Eccl 12:6,7 "or ever the silver cord be loosed or the golden bowl be broken or the pitcher be broken at the cistern. Then shall the dust return to earth as it was and the spirit shall return unto God who gave it".

One hot afternoon the woman of Samira embarked on a short journey to simply get waters for domestic use from the well and get back home she was not in anticipation of any event or to meet any personality since she does not have any child or perhaps a maid, it is the normal routine for her to go to the well and fetch water and return back uneventful, but this particular day without her knowledge became a day heaven ordained to bring her in as an apostle in the market place.

It was not her encounter with Jesus that made her an apostle in the market place, it was her response to the said encounter that made her an apostle in the market place.

When she left her home, she did not plan to preach to anybody about Jesus. She went to her normal domestic chores but in the process of her normal activities as a full housewife, she had encounter that changed her life and her destiny.

See John 4:6-7 "Now Jacob's well was there. Jesus therefore being wearied with his journey sat thou on the well and it was about the sixth hour. There cometh a woman of Samira to draw water. Jesus saith unto her, give me to drink". The woman was doing normal duty of every house wife simply to draw water. Story about the woman of Samaria going home with her pot of water was never mentioned. The main reason she came to the well was never mentioned why because she entered her calling, the reason for her existence, the main reason God brought her to the well.

Jesus asked her to give him water to drink because Jesus knew that the woman of Samira had the tool and the ability to give him the water.

Initially the woman taught Jesus was asking the ordinary water but when she realized the kind of water Jesus was looking for.

She realized it is not the water in the well that Jesus was asking for, and the thirsty of Jesus cannot be quenched with the water from the well and the real disciples of Jesus have not known the kind of water Jesus need and the kind of meat Jesus was desiring for.

In John 4:28-30 "The woman then left her water pot, and went her way into the city, and saith to the men, come see a man, which told me all things that ever I did. Is not this the Christ? Then they went out of the city, and came unto him".

Jesus is still telling you that he is thirsty and he had need for a meat. Are you prepared to quench Jesus thirst and hunger for meat. Do you want to be like the woman of Samaria that fulfilled Jesus thirst and hunger or do you want to be like the disciples of Jesus that went in search of food (money) rather than in search of souls (the real meat).

It was a Sunday like today (7th December 2014 my wedding anniversary as I was in New York writing part of this book) a single woman that was not married left her home that early morning to the church (synagogue) but to the cemetery. One would have wondered what a single lady is doing at a cemetery on a Sunday morning. She would look like somebody who was demented, if accosted on the way and she will say that she is going to the grave yard with spices to a dead body that was dead for three days.

But don't blame her, she did not even know that she has a destiny to fulfill. She did not know that heaven was waiting for her to be enlisted in her record as a carrier of good news of resurrection.

In John 20:1 "The first day of the week cometh Mary Magdalene early, when it was yet dark unto the sepulcher and seeth the stone taken away from the sepulcher".

What Mary saw was beyond her imagination and expectation; she went to the tomb with simple desire to see her dead master and drop her spice to his tomb, perhaps cry a little, console herself and then go back to face her life.

But what Mary was today was not that she left her house when it was yet dark, it was not because she saw that the stone had been taken away from the tomb, it is also not because she ran to call Simon Peter. She would have done all these things without fulfilling her destiny. Heaven may not have recorded it for her.

If she had ended up running to Simon Peter to alert him that the stone had been taken away. After alerting them, she did not run to her home or go to the city to announce to them that the stone had been removed.

She followed the disciples back to the tomb to know what must have happened to the body of her master she loved even when the master was dead.

What Mary became was as a result of a single perseverance to show love to the dead master without knowing or realizing that the master had risen from the dead.

John 20:11 "But Mary stood without at the sepulcher weeping and as she wept, she stooped down, and looked into the sepulcher."

While others have abandoned their place and function at the market place but Mary stood without at the place of her divine encounter and divine assignment.

It was this Mary's attitude to the calling of God upon her life that brought the incident in John 20:17 "Jesus saith unto her touch me not for I am not yet ascended, and say unto them, I ascend unto my father, and your father and to my God and your God".

Mary on this fateful day did not leave her house as an apostle but by the end of the day by her action she was ordained an apostle, by becoming a carrier of the good news of Jesus resurrection.

Elisha as a prophet of God did not go through school of prophet, he was not among the sons of the prophet recorded in the bible. He was nothing but a big time farmer, who concentrated on his farm.

On this fateful day, Elisha was not in the synagogue. He woke up as it was normal for him and left for his farming work. He did not invite any visitor and was not expecting any one at the farm. If any visitor should come, it should be in the evening when he has finished his farming activities.

But it is not in your hand to decide where and when God will choose to visit you. What matters is not where God visited you. It could be in the farm, in the office, in the market, the hospital or the tomb like Mary Magdalene, what matters most is your response to the said divine encounter.

In 2 King 19:19 "So he departed thence and found Elisha the son of Shaphat who was plowing with twelve yoke oxen before him, and he with the twelfth and Elijah passed by him and cast his mantle upon him".

Elisha was not praising God or praying when Elijah met him, he was simply doing what every big time farmer was doing. There was not expectation of call of God upon his life because he was not among the sons of the prophet. Elisha was doing his normal professional job when the call to serve God came upon him as an apostle of God in the old testament.

Today that you are a farmer, businessman or woman or civil servant is not excuse that God cannot call you into the market place.

Everything depend upon your response to God's invitation to be used by Him to work for him as an apostle in the market place.

In Esther 4:8 "Also he gave him the copy of the writing of the decree that was given at Shushan to destroy them, to show it unto Esther, and to decrees it unto her, and to charge her that she should go in unto the King, to make supplication unto him, and to make request before him for her people".

The above scripture is the mandate given by Mordecai to Esther to go in and see the King.

One does not need to tell Esther to go in and see the king because it is her daily chore except the days the king does not want her to come.
What is in it to ask a full house wife to go and see the husband whether he is a king or not. Esther by this time has become the queen of the kingdom as the husband was the king.

But there was a demand that it is time to tell the king that Esther was a Jew (born again Christian). Perhaps Esther have been hiding her identity as a captive. But event to show if she can honour God and forget her ego or pride came.

Some of us who have been hiding our identity in our place of work or neighbourhood, time has come for us to show who we are and we are confused because we have been hiding our identity.

Esther like every other house wife must have slept with the husband and wake to receive a message from Mordecai to go in to the king to save life.

Esther did not marry the king to teach the king how to pray to the God of Esther. She did not marry the king to enthrone the practice of law of Moses in that kingdom.

After her marriage to the king she had resumed her normal house wife responsibility to the husband until this fateful day God was looking for ordinary person (house wife inclusive) to enlist to be God's apostles in the market place to save lives of God's people.

Esther did not respond to Mordecai to say that she came to marry not to go into supplication to the king on behalf of the Jews. But she saw opportunity to appreciate God for all that God had done for her from being an orphan to becoming a queen in a foreign land. she did not abdicate the assignment God gave her because she was not a world renounced intercessors.

What are you presently doing now is enough for God to use it to enlist you as an apostle at the market place with simple responsibility to save lives either through preaching or intercession.

Daniel did not go to Babylon as a prophet, he went there like any other captive brought from Israel. In Daniel 5:13 "Then was Daniel brought in before the king. And the King spake and said unto Daniel that thou Daniel, which art of the children of the captivity of Judah, whom the children of the captivity of Judah, who the king my father brought out of Jewry".

Daniel did not announce to anybody that he is a prophet of God, the only thing that qualified Daniel at the beginning of his captivity he purpose in his heart not to defile himself which resulted in excellent spirit of God dwelling in him.

See how Daniel was described in Daniel 5:11 "There is a man in thy kingdom, in whom is the Spirit of the holy gods, and in the days of thy father light and understanding and wisdom like the wisdom of the gods, was found in him whom the king Nebuchadnezzar thy father, the king, I say thy father made master of the magicians, astrologers, Chaldeans, and soothsayers".

Does the spirit of the Holy God dwell in you? Then you are qualified to give life to people both in the kingdom of God and kingdom of Babylon.

Daniel qualification was not that he was a priest, he was an administrator by profession and was engaged by the Babylonian government as an administrator.

But what made Daniel different from the other administrators that the excellent spirit was found in him.

Daniel was only called after the main magicians, astrologers have failed to do what they were trained to do.

That fateful day Daniel resumed work as an administrator like others but there was a problem in the palace which administrative skill could not handle.

Daniel did not ask God to give the king a dream that he will forget. Daniel used what God gave him to function as an apostle in the market place. You are that ordinary person doing your normal professional job or work but God will use you in that place of work to give life to people, to share the love and mercy of God through Jesus Christ to people.

The maid to Naaman's wife was caught as a captive and was assigned to serve Naaman's wife. See 2 Kg. 5:2 "An d the Syrians had gone out by companies and had brought away captive out of the land of Israel a little maid, and she waited on Naaman's wife."

The description of Naaman's maid was that she was brought as a captive from the land of Israel, she was also a little maid with a responsibility to wait on Naaman's wife.

It was during the time she was performing her duty to Naaman's wife she discovered that the master was leprous and remembered that he can receive cure from God of Israel.

The little maid did not go to Syria on her own volition, she went there as a captive not as a pastor or an apostle. She resumed her job as a maid unto Naaman's wife, not Naaman's wife pastor or prophet.

In the course of doing her normal duty, that is serving Naaman's wife she saw a need in the life of Naaman and decided to introduce Naaman to the God that can give him life and healing at the same time.

Today that little maid, the bible did not describe her little the maid was, but though she was little her faith was not little and she knows that her God is not little.

That you are a captive were you are living or working does not stop you from been God's representative there. Are you a maid, employee, employer, visitor, gardener, driver or whatever is your normal profession is not an excuse to stop your function as an apostle at the market place.

We maybe embittered by the condition we found ourselves in the place of work, or any other place there is no reason why we should not represent God and give life to people or introduce them to the love and mercy of God.

Nehemiah was nothing but the kings cup bearer see Neh. 1 :11 "O Lord, I beseech thee, let now thine ear be attentive to the prayer of thy servant, and to the prayer of the servants, who desire to fear thy name, and prosper, I pray thee, thy servant this day, and grant him mercy in the sight of this man. For I was the king's cup bearer".

Today we have read the book of Nehemiah stating his account with the king, he served and his role in rebuilding the walls of Jerusalem that had been broken down.

Nehemiah did not see himself only as king's cup bearer. He did not relax in his comfort zone as personal assistant to the king or the king chief of staff.

When Nehemiah saw the need of his people in the market place he can use his position as king's cup bearer to secure a release for his people, he did not play down on it.

One thing that is common to all these apostles in the market place. They were men and women engaged in the ordinary things some of us are involved with but responded to the need of the people today they are known beyond their ordinary profession or work but are known as men and women God used to introduce himself and show his greatness.

We can be like all these men and women whom the Lord used to change history.

Moses was quite busy taking care of his father inlaws's business when God met him in the burning bush and gave him an assignment which he responded immediately.

Remember that God did not throw down any mantle or rod to Moses from heaven. It was the same rod Moses made for himself to control his father inlaw's flock that God used to do wonders in Egypt. It is the same rod God used to divide the red sea. See Ex. 4:2 "And the Lord said unto him what is that in thine hand? And he said a rod". In Ex. 3:1 "Now Moses kept theflock of Jethro his father inlaw, the priest of Midian and he led the flock to the backside of the desert, and came to the mountain of God even to Horeb"

One begin to wonder why God should prefer a shepherd man, an employee of his father inlaw to a priest of Midian. Moses father inlaw was already a priest, an employer of labour, married with one wife and grown up daughters, but God for the assignment he preferred a professional rather than a priest.

This is the same priest that visited Moses and gave him advise on leadership which Moses followed. It means that Moses father inlaw was not devoid of wisdom on leadership but God did not choose him but chose Moses.

Have you left your position as an apostle in the market place to take up a priestly position which God did not appoint you, but man or your G. O appointed you. Well you will remain irrelevant in the agenda of God in the dispensation or assignment God is using apostles in the market place.

We are not deriding any pastor or priestly position, they are needed by God and needed in the body of Christ. But the point here is that if God had not called you as a priest (pastor) and you found yourself there by your personal desire or nomination by man without appointment coming from God, it is better you move to where God has called you.

I have a friend who was a pastor in charge of a branch of one of the Pentecostal churches in Nigeria. After some years working as a pastor he realized that was not the place of his calling.

He quickly resigned and started bus evangelism, today he is fulfilled he has sons and daughters in the Lord all over the country. He ministered to different people on daily basis.

Since he started the bus evangelism 7 years ago over 1,000 souls have given their lives through his ministration.

Both the priest is important as well as the professional doing God's assignment in the place of his work or business referred to as apostle in the market place.

The day David fought Goliath he went with his catapult and food on his head not with any sword or weapon.

He did not go there with any intention to fight Goliath, he went there on domestic assignment his father gave him to do in 1 Sam 17:17, 18 "And Jesse said unto David his son take now for thy brethren an ephah of this parched corn, and these ten loaves, and run to the camp to thy brethren. And carry these ten cheese unto the captain of their thousand, and look how thy brethren fare, and take their pledge".

David went there as an errand boy for his father. He was not trained as a soldier (pastor or priest) he was a shepherd boy. 1 Sam 17:15 "But David went and returned from Saul to feed his father's sheep at Bethlehem?"

It was David elder brothers that are trained soldiers that went to war with Saul 1 Sam. 17:13,14 "And the three eldest sons Jesse went and followed Saul to the battle …. And David was the youngest, and three eldest followed Saul."

What happened at the battle ground does not require the intervention of a shepherd boy, it only requires a trained professional soldier because the enemy of Israel Goliath, have been fighting from his youth, just like the devil have deceiving the world before some of us were born.

But when the contention came on board, when it became obvious that the children of Israel need to be saved, God had given opportunity for trained professional soldiers for 40 days to contend with Goliath but they were all afraid.

After 40 days of God's waiting for the trained to do what he needed, God was compelled to look for a young lad who was not professionally trained, to fight his battle and liberate his people from the hands of Goliath.

It is not the training God is looking for now. What God needs are those who will have enough confidence in the ability of God and carry out his function at the market place.

The battle fought in 1 Sam. 17 was not fought in the synagogue or church it was the battle in the market palace.

That battle against Goliath in the market place have not ceased, only there are not willing professional or businessmen or women who will volunteer to fight the Goliath in the market place and liberate so many souls that have became captives to the tricks and devices of the kingdom of darkness.

We the apostles in the market place cannot afford to shirk our responsibilities there. Infact it will be disastrous if the apostles in the market becomes afraid like the trained soldiers of Saul.

The same fear and boasting Goliath exhibited and put inside the children of Israel is still being experienced now in the market place. Many believers who have become entangled with civilian affairs have lost the grip to fight like soldiers.

Compromise among the apostles in the market place have made so many of us to bury our face in shame and lost the propelling power to contend for our faith in the market place.

But the dry bones must rise again and anytime a dry bone rises it must become exceeding army.

It does not matter where the enemy has cornered you and subdued you with sin, compromise, bribery and corruption, immorality, anger, depression, abortion and murder.

God is still waiting for you to take up your position and your responsibility in the market place and minister the love and mercy of God through Christ Jesus to people.

All these professionals mentioned in this chapter also had one issue or the other but when the call of God came for them to arise and be indeed the apostles in the market place they did not decline but rather accepted the offer and today their names have become a reference point.

Even in our contemporary society where we lived, we have various men and women who did not start as a pastor but started as professionals before God called them into full time ministry or apostles in the market place

Men like Arc. Ifeanyi Odedo, an architect by profession and owner of hotels today is working for God in the market place under the Full Gospel Businessmen Fellowship.

Arc. Azike Diribe, Arc. Bunmi Adedeji, Engr. Okeoma Agu, Engr. Toks Obayan, Barr. Boss Mustapha, Mr. David Maseli, Pharm. Ngozi Okoronkwo, Mr. Akin Oludimi, Dr. Segun Falope, Dr. Nicholas Iragunima, Elder Onoh .O. Onoh, Deacon Festus Nwokafor, Prof. Mike Onyekonwu, Engr. Andrew Essien and so many that there would not be enough space to mention here. They are professionals but are working for God in the market place.

Apart from those working for God in the market place. Some of the general overseer of some renowned churches started as professionals like Pastor E. A. Adeboye has a Phd in mathematics as a senior lecturer in the university, Dr. David Oyedepo of Living Faith ministries, Pastor Kumuyi of Deeper Life Christian church was also a lecturer before he became a full time Pastor, Barr. Emeka Nwankpa and some of these G. O. are architects, doctors and lawyers etc.

God have not stopped calling professionals or businessmen into his divine agenda. Identify the area God has called you, and apply yourself to it and make full proof of your calling.

Your entrance does not determine your end is what you do with your entrance into God's purpose that determines your end.

Are you a professional or businessman or woman, you are equally important to God to be used as well as a priest or pastor is important to God.

Your congregation and your church is in the place of your work or business only utilize every opportunity God have given you to minister his love and mercy through Christ Jesus to people you come in contact every day.

Your life is not complete until you combine your business or work with God's agenda for your life. You will not be living your life to fullness until you add to it the function of winning souls to God through Jesus Christ.

Barrister Favour Victory

CHAPTER THREE

THE ROLES OF THE APOSTLES IN THE MARKET PLACE

God has different roles for the apostle in the market place. It is essential you discover the role God had assigned to you so that you can profit from it.

There is always a reward for a successful completion of God's assignment in 1 Sam. 17:26 "And David spake to the men that stood by him, saying, what shall be done to the man that killeth this philistine, and taketh away the reproach from Israel? For who is this uncircumcised Philistine, that he should defy the armies of the living God?

For every successful completion of the assignment of the apostle in the market place, three things are obvious to take place, the first is the instrument God used shall be rewarded as David was rewarded by the king. The second thing is that reproach shall be taken away from God's children and the third thing God's name shall be glorified.

So there are various functions or assignment God gives out to the apostles in the market place but the end result of all of them is to save life and manifest the glory of God.

These functions are equal importance to God and reward the same see Matt. 25:15 – 23 "And unto one he gave five talents, to another two, and to another one, to every man according to his several ability, and straightway took his journey" His Lord said unto him well done, good and faithful servant, thou hast been faithful over a few things, I will make thee ruler over many things, enter thou into the joy of the Lord".

We will be looking at different responsibilities God had given to his apostles in the market place, though this list is not exhaustive but we may consider a few.

a. PREACHING THE WORD OF GOD

in Acts 1:8 "But ye shall receive power, after that the Holy Ghost is come upon you an ye shall be witnesses unto me both in Jerusalem and in all Judea, and in Samaria, and unto the uttermost part of the earth".

Also in Matt. 28:19-20 "Go ye therefore and teach all nations baptizing them in the name of the father, and of the son and of the Holy Ghost. Teaching them to observe all things whatsoever I have commanded you and lo I am with you always even unto the end of the world. Amen".

This is a command God gave to his apostles and these command has not changed.

The bible recorded that after the apostles received the commandment from God they went forward to carry out God instructions.

In Mark 16:19-20 "So then after the Lord had spoken unto them, he was received up into heaven, and sat on the right hand of God. And they went froth, and preached everywhere, the Lord working with them, and conforming the word with signs following Amen."

If the apostles did not step out to preach everywhere, God would not have stepped out to work with them and the signs and wonders that followed their ministry would not have been seen.

God did no step out to work with them because they have apostle as a title or they have been with Jesus, the only reason God can step out to work with any person be it a man or woman or even a child is only when that person that is obedient to God's command goes out to preach.

The bible recorded that the apostles preached everywhere. It means that it was not only in the synagogue they preached. They preached everywhere means everywhere. Anywhere souls could be found whether in the office, business premises, hospitals, companies, market, parks, trade fair, restaurant, hotel and so on.

Today we have limited our preaching to church and even required how many hours church service will last.

If it was only to come and die Jesus would not have spent 33½ years on earth. But he knew that the essence of his coming to the earth is most importantly to die and secondly recruit men who will go everywhere to preach the good news of Jesus death and the salvation it brought to every man kind.

In Luke 5:10 "And Jesus said unto Simon, fear not, from henceforth thou shalt catch men".

Jesus is telling every believer that from henceforth thou shall catch men.

He is telling every apostle in the market place that henceforth thou shall catch men.

Are you catching men and women or are you just busy acquiring wealth, catching money, contract and promotion without catching the men that work with you, do business with you, living in your neighourhood, entering the same plane, bus or train with you.

God is calling every believer to start now to fulfill his or her primary assignment by witnessing him where he works or do business or live.

Jesus has informed us that the harvest is plenteous and labourers are few. Why not increase the labourers and be part of God's agenda in this end time.

In 1 Cor. 9:16-17 "Fear though I preach the gospel, I have nothing to glory of **for necessity is laid upon me,** yea, woe is unto me, If I preach not the gospel for if **I do this thing willingly, I have a reward:** but if against my will, a dispensation of the gospel is committed unto me".

We all have a responsibility to all men we come across in our life to preach the word of God or share our testimony of God's faithfulness.

In Rev. 22:12 "And behold I come quickly, and my reward is with me, to give every man according as his work shall be".

The issue of preaching as a responsibility to every believer is a mandatory assignment given by God, it is only when you step out to fulfill this divine mandate that God will step out to work wonders with you and that is when heaven will recognize you as an apostle.

Every believer who utilizes opportunities that comes to him or her to preach the word of God to people and perhaps God using them convert such one from his sin is indeed an apostle in the market place. He has fulfilled the same thing the apostles of Jesus did in Mark 16 and went everywhere to preach the word of God.

To start preaching does not require knowing all the scriptures in the bible. You can share the love of God as expressed in **John 3:16** God loved everybody and does not want anybody to perish and miss eternal life and go to hell.

b. Healing

In **Acts 10:38** "How God anointed Jesus of Nazareth with the Holy Ghost and with power: who went about doing good, and **healing** all that were oppressed of the devil, for God was with him".

It is important to note that every one that is sick needs healing irrespective of the kind of sickness or disease. Every one that is sick is being oppressed by the devil.

Part of the reason why Jesus came was to heal us from every disease and sickness and to deliver us from the oppression of the devil.

When Jesus was here on earth, the bible recorded that He went about doing good and healing all that were oppressed by the devil. Jesus movement of healing people was not limited in the synagogue (church), he went about means he moved from places to places wherever souls of men that are sick could be found, wherever souls of men oppressed by the devil, Jesus saw them as his own congregation and ministered healing to them.

Jesus has commanded us the believers to do the same he did in Mark 16:17-18 "And these signs shall follow them that believe in my name shall cast out devils, they shall speak with new tongues, they shall take up serpents, and if they drink any deadly thing, it shall not hurt them, they shall lay hands on the sick and they shall recover".

Also in James 5:14-15 "Is any sick among you? Let him call for the elder of the church, and let them pray over him anointing him with the oil in the name of the Lord. And the prayer of faith shall save the sick, and the Lord shall raise him up, and if he have committed sins, they shall be forgiven him"

I have discovered that healing has become a platform for so many people. Testimonies abound of people who receive salvation as a result of their ill health. When any man is sick and being on the danger of death or fear of death, ask him or her to reject Satan and embrace Jesus he will willingly do that.

My late mother gave her life to Christ when she was sick. I saw it as an opportunity to lead her to Christ. I led her to Christ and thereafter prayed for her. She lived few more years and died and I have believe that she made heaven.

My mother in law gave her life to Christ when she became sick. One of our ministers friend came to pray for her and asked her whether she will like to give her life to Christ and she accepted.

She was prayed for and led to Christ when some of her children came to visit her in our home she was telling them that she has given her life to Jesus.

I remember an experience I had some years back in my office. I am a lawyer by profession and have my legal firm. There was this Muslim family I was handling a land case for them in the court, they were three most elder ones in their family that comes to my office in respect to the case. And anytime they come I normally give them a Christian magazine called voice magazine of the full gospel businessmen fellowship international Nigeria.

One of these days they visited me and the eldest among them over 70 years of old complained to me that he has been sick for a while. I asked him if he wouldn't mind, I pray for him and he accepted. In the process of praying for his healing, I asked them if they will be willing to give their lives to Jesus and the two of them that came that day accepted. In my office I led two of them to Christ and prayed for them.

Everyone needs healing whether a Christian, a heathen, Muslim, Buddhist or atheist. No one ever reject the gift of prayer for healing because everyone wants to stay alive, nobody wants to die.

Jesus has given us a tremendous power to use and give life to people and thereafter give them eternal life.

Every opportunity to pray for someone to be healed is another greater opportunity to give the person salvation on a platter of Gold. Majority of them do not reject of the offer of salvation when they are sick.

Sickness is an oppression from the devil and God has given us the power and the mandate to kick devil out of the lives of those around us.

Recently I was travelling from Port Harcourt to Lagos, at the airport I met a Christian lady that I knew, she was also travelling to a different destination but she complained to me that she was sick. At the departure hall of the airport in the midst of the crowd waiting to board their flight, I prayed for her and God healed her.

It does not matter the environment once somebody is sick he only needs solution to his problem, ask the mighty man of valour Naaman, he was not interested in whom suggested were he can get healing, all he needs is healing. When somebody needs healing tell him to dip himself 7 times in the sea, he will do it all he needs is to receive healing.

If Naaman with all his pedigree should accept to do what Elisha asked him to do, there is nobody who would not want to receive Jesus into his life as long as he will be healed.

As apostles in the market place let's utilize the power and privilege God has given to us through Jesus.

But remember that prayer for healing without a corresponding gift of salvation to the person is not complete and healthy, because every sick person who became healed will still die and if he is not born again will go to hell.

Healing is only an attraction to lead people to God through Jesus Christ. Any healing that did not end in salvation is not complete.

As apostle in the market place we have been anointed with power to pray for healing for anybody and he will receive it. We need to have confidence in ourselves and faith in God that once we pray for people they will be healed. Jesus has made provision for our healing in 1 Peter 2:24 "Who his own self bare our sins in his own body on the tree, that we, being dead to sins, should live unto righteousness by whose stripes ye were healed".

Jesus had made provision, it is our responsibility as the apostles in the market place to enforce it and encourage our neighbours, colleagues and client or customer to receive this free gift of healing coming from our Lord Jesus.

We as apostles in the market place always challenge people around us in faith any time we make ourselves available for God to use and heal people. It is our responsibility to inform them they can receive it.

There are a lot of examples in the bible where Paul a lawyer, God used him mightily to heal many. It came to a point the lawyer turned apostles, apron from his body were healing people.

Peter a professional fisherman when he became an apostle of Jesus, the healing virtue flowing from him was so great that his shadow was healing people.

Are you a professional like Paul and Peter or a business man; you can still be used by God to heal and win souls for the kingdom of God.

    c. **Prayer:**

In Luke 18:1 "And he spake a parable unto them to this end that men ought always to pray, and not to faint".
In 1 Thess. 5:17 "Pray without ceasing". An apostle in the market place cannot accomplish much if he does not pray. Prayer is key if you must fulfill your purpose as an apostle in the market place.

The type of prayer required in this is about 3 dimensional.
The first is prayer for yourself to be strong to accomplish what God had given you to do for him in the market place, the second type of prayer is a prayer you pray for others call intercession and supplication for their need. The third type of prayer is a prayer to God enforcing the purpose of God in heaven here on earth. Jesus said in Matt. 6:10 "Thy kingdom come. Thy will be done in earth, as it is in heaven".

The importance of prayer as a function and as being part of apostleship was emphasized by Jesus so much that the apostles requested that He should teach them how to pray in Luke 11:1 "And it came to pass, that as he was praying in a certain place when .. he ceased one of his disciples said unto him, God teach us to pray, as John also taught his disciples".

We know that in our contemporary society God had raised so many apostles in the market place with sole responsibility of leading intercessors in this continent and teaching pastors and apostles in the market place in the area of intercession, men like Barr. Emeka Nwankpa, Engr. Steve Olumuyiwa, Engr. Victor Uchegbulam and Dr. Johnny Uhuegbu.

As an apostle in the market place, it is a responsibility God had given to us to pray on all manners of issues affecting people we encounter in the field.

Last year we organize a market place outreach during a trade fair, organized in the city I live. In one of the outreaches a military man attended our outreaches, when we called for people who need to be prayed for he came out and I prayed for him. As I was praying for him, God led me in my heart to pray for his trip and pray for divine protection. The military man after the prayer thanked me and told me that in the next few days he will be leaving the country for a peace corps mission outside the country. He went to thank the man that invited him to the outreach.

This is an area God is greatly using my good friend Mr. Jacob John that lives in London in United Kingdom. God uses him greatly in the place of prayer for people. God gives him personal ministration for people as he prays for them. Testimonies abound both in Nigeria, in UK and other nations, where God had used him tremendously in the place of prayer. He is also one of the apostles in the market place in this dispensation.

This is the ministry people like Esther function effectively when the lives of her people were in danger in Esther 4:16 : "Go, gather together all the Jews that are present in Shushan, and fast ye for me, and neither eat nor drink three days, night or day. I also and my maidens will fast likewise, and so will I go in unto the king, which is not according to the law: and if I perish, I perish".

The battle Esther won as an ap0stle in the market place was done through prayer. We have discovered that every apostle in the market place who engages the force of prayer can change any situation no matter how difficult it appears.

Nehemiah was the king's cup bearer but it was the force of prayer he used to accomplish God's purpose and assignment for him.

The position of being king's cup bearer was designed by God for Nehemiah to use it and accomplish God's purpose for his life. In Neh. 2:4-5a "Then the king said unto me, for what dost thou make request? So I prayed to the God of heaven. And I said unto the king…"
Nehemiah prays to God first before he speaks unto the king. He knew that once a matter is settled before God no hindrance can stand on the way.

Nehemiah used the ministry of prayer as an apostle in the market place to accomplish God's assignment to him. Men like Daniel are examples of apostles in the market place who used the ministry of prayer to achieve God's divine agenda in their life.

Part of the function of the Apostles in the market place is to engage the force of prayer to bring people to the knowledge of truth and receive salvation from God.

d. Sharing testimonies:
The greatest weapon of an apostle in the market place is his testimonies. It could be testimony of his salvation or testimony of his healing or testimony of business breakthrough.

Those testimonies of how you got admission and graduate is what God is waiting for you to share with others. The testimony of how you married or get your present job is what is needed to convince people in the market place to give their lives to Christ.

Those in the market place understand that you are not a pastor or trained minister of God, so if you don't share any scripture you will be pardoned but share what you have, the one you don't need any training before you share.

The testimony of how you started your business or how many years you waited before your wife conceive and had children. All those people out there are waiting to hear you. Any close mouth of God's goodness limit his destiny sometimes they said closed mouth is closed destiny.

The issue is that the more you share your testimony the more God gives you more testimonies to share.

A Muslim or heathen many not want to hear your preaching, your prayer or collect Christian magazine from you, but they must listen when you begin to share your life story of God's goodness.

As apostles in the market place sharing a testimony is not an option. It is a requirement from Jesus when He told us that we are going to be His witnesses. In Acts 1:8b "..And ye shall be witnesses unto me both in Jerusalem, and in all Judea, and Samaria, and unto the uttermost part of the earth."

God expect us as his apostles in the market place to witness for him, his love and mercy.

The woman of Samaria understood it immediately she encountered Jesus and went into action in John 4:28-30 "The woman then left her water pot, and went her way into the city, and said to the men, come, see a man, which told me all things that ever I did. Is not this the Christ? Then they went out of the city, and come unto him".

The resultant effect of sharing testimonies are great see John 4:41-42 "And many more believed because of his own word. And said unto the woman, now we believe, not because of thy saying: For we have heard him ourselves and know that this is indeed the Christ, the savior of the world".

This is a great tool the men of Full Gospel Business Fellowship International all over the world had used for the past 60 years the fellowship had been in existence and have drawn thousands or millions of souls to the kingdom of God for the years past.

It is a tool the fellowship is still using and achieving great result in winning souls and fulfilling God's purpose. The foundation of the fellowship is Jesus but the major method of the fellowship evangelical means is the use of sharing testimonies both in convention and normal fellowship meeting.

Every apostle in the market place that is a member of the Full Gospel Businessmen Fellowship can attest to what God had used the testimonies of members or invited guest to do in the life of people all around the world.

God knows the power and effect of testimonies in the lives of people at the beginning of the Fellowship of Full Gospel Businessmen Fellowship International; he mandated them to reduce people's testimonies in a Christian magazine called voice.

This voice that contains the testimonies of apostles in the market place has became a very great tools in the hand of these apostles in winning souls and fulfilling God's mandate to us. Several souls have been won by simply sharing of voice magazine to people.

Everybody has a testimony to share there is nobody that do not have a testimony to share.

If the woman of Samaria with a terrible past should have testimony there is nobody that does not have a testimony. The enemy started on time to mess up the testimony of the woman of Samaria. She had been separated from 4 husbands, currently known as husband snatcher. She had suffered from childlessness for the period of cohabiting with many men. She had suffered from lack that was why she always desired to live with a man that will foot her bills.

It does not matter how the devil had messed up you to look like a cheap harlot or poor person within your neighbourhood, God is still ready to turn your mess to your message.

The same thing the devil denied the woman of Samaria, a child, is the same thing God used to encounter her and turned her story from a husband snatcher to apostle in the market place.

It is quite obvious that if that woman was blessed with a child for this period of her living with different men, her child would have been a grown up child. She wouldn't have been at the well to fetch water that would have been the domestic responsibility of her child. If that had happened, she would have missed the opportunity of meeting Jesus at the well, perhaps she would have died unsong(not celebrated).

I remember a story a friend of mine shared with me. It was Christmas season, they did not have enough money to travel with their children and they decided to celebrate the Christmas in the rented apartment they were living then.

On this fateful day when others have travelled, she sat in front of their rented apartment with nothing to do, a man walk to her and said he was looking for her, because the man was a stranger, she inquired from the man the reason why he was looking for her without introducing herself. It was then the man said I am looking for the person because I have her employment letter to deliver to her.

To cut the long story short, it was that letter of employment with a multinational oil company that changed the fortune of the family till today. No matter how bad your past has been, God can still use it to convert people.

The woman of Samaria didn't say much, did not say how much she had made, how many children she had received, but simply said come and see the person who have told me everything about me, could he be the Christ.

When the people of the city came they also believed because they also encountered Jesus.

When you share your testimony, you bring them or create a platform for them to encounter God through Jesus Christ.

God is depending upon your testimony to bring that soul to him. Share it.

e. Giving Out Alms:

Giving are topics people don't like to hear about especially those who have not understood the importance of giving in the life of a Christian.

In Gen. 12:2 "And I will make of thee a great nation, and I will bless thee, and make thy name great, and thou shalt be a blessing"

The essence of God blessing his children is also to make them a blessing to others. We are blessed to bless. For every act of giving in the bible was recorded either offering by a widow in the synagogue or giving to people. In Acts 10:1-2 "There was a certain man in Ceasarea called Cornelius, a centurion of the brand called the Italian bans, a devout man, and one that feared God with all his house, which gave much alms to the people, and prayed to God always".

The Cornelius gave much alms to the people but his relationship with God remain intact. It means that it is the love from God that flows into his heart that moves him to give alms to the people.

Giving alms without a corresponding relationship with, do not have any solid foundation. No matter the level of your giving if you are not born again, you do not have a relationship with God; you are not qualified to be called the apostle in the market place.

It goes further to mean that every believer who is a devout Christian has a responsibility to engage in the act of giving.

The giving here means giving to people and giving to support the kingdom of God.

Today it is quite obvious that to propagate the kingdom of God, money is needed. We have many people who are Christians that are rich but find it difficult to support crusades, outreaches, conventions and evangelical programmes.

I am particular touched about the act of most terrorist group operating in the world. There are people who believe in their cause and spend millions to finance such group. Among this group there are those that do not have money to finance the group but they volunteer their lives to be suicide bombers.

This should serve as a great challenge to all of us that are Christians. If you don't have money to give for God's work you can give your service, you can give your life. God desires the best because He has given His best in John 3:16 "For God so lived the world that He gave His only begotten son, that whosoever believeth in him should not perish, but have everlasting life".

We are called to give so that we can be given as the bible stated in Luke 6:38 "Give and it shall be given unto you. Good measure, pressed down, and shaken together, and running over, shall men give into your bosom. For with the same measure that ye mete withal it shall be measured to you again".

We are not dwelling primarily on giving but it is important we know that every apostle in the market place is called to giving. This giving may be money, time, service, material things or love to the hurting world or to the needy.

Don't neglect giving if you want your testimony to abound in the market place. God had called you into market place to bless you abundantly, give God a platform to do it effectively.

f. Interpreting Dreams:

Many Christians do not have this gift but if you don't have it remain committed in the area of your own calling.

But we have seen through the scriptures that this is a gift that God had used to elevate some apostles in the market place. For eg Joseph in Gen 40:8 "And they said unto him, we have dreamed a dream, and there is no interpreter of it. And Joseph said unto them, do not interpretations belongs to God? Tell me them I pray you".

Joseph utilized this gift when he saw that his fellow prisoners were looking moody. The interpretation he gave them was accurate to the point and within few days there was a manifestation of those dreams according to the interpretation of Joseph.

Joseph did not go about looking for people that he wants to interpret their dreams. He only responded to the act of feeling concern for his fellow prisoners when he saw them looking moody.

Those in your office or neighbourhood looking sad or moody needs a caring concern from you as apostle in the market place. You may have the gift of interpretation of dreams but because there is no opportunity to express it or manifest it, you may not know that you have the gift.

That time in prison was the first recorded Joseph interpreted a dream. The other time he dreamed and shared his dream. The bible did not say Joseph interpreted his dream to his brothers though he understood the meaning of the dream.

It is this gift of interpretation that was expressed in the life of Joseph that when Pharaoh had a dream and was looking for somebody to interpret the dream Joseph was recommended by pharaoh's servant.

In Gen 41:12-13 "And there was there with us a young man, an Hebrew, servant to the captain of the guard, and we told him, and he interpreted to us our dreams to each man according to his dream he did interpret. And it came to pass, as he interpreted to us, so it was, me he resorted unto mine office, and him he hanged".

Also in Gen 41:25 "And Joseph said unto Pharaoh, the dream of Pharaoh is one God had showed pharaoh what he is about to do".

Daniel is another apostle in the market place God used with the gift of interpretation of dreams Dan. 5:11, 12 "There is a man in thy kingdom, in whom is the spirit of the holy gods, and in the days of thy father light and understanding and wisdom, like the wisdom of the gods, was found in him, whom the king Nebuchadnezzar thy father, the king, I say, thy father, made master of the magicians astrologers, Chaldeans and soothsayers, for as much as an excellent spirit, and knowledge, and understanding interpreting of dreams and showing of hand sentences and dissolving of doubts, were found in the same Daniel."

By the gift of interpretation of dream hard things in the life of people are dissolved. The confusion people experienced after such terrible nightmare is handled.

It is important to realize that the gift of interpreting dreams are not ordinary gift. The spiritual controls the physical. Sometimes it is through dreams we receive information of what devil is about to do in our life and we call it nightmare. Sometimes God speak to us through dreams as he spoke to Joseph and Solomon.

So as an apostle in the market place if you have discovered this gift in you ensure that you utilize it effectively. Kings in the bible became converted through interpretation of dreams.

What do you expect from a king that dreamt and forget his dream and need somebody to remember the dream for him and interpret it. It is only what God can do and this is enough to enthrone God in that kingdom.

The end result of this gift is that the name of God may be glorified. All those God used in the bible to interpret dreams like Joseph and Daniel were all apostles in the market place.

The gift you have if properly utilized will still achieve the same result somebody called to preaching, healing or prayer ministry.

The end result of the activities of the apostle in the market place is to seek avenue and use the gift God has given to him to draw people to God.

g. **Contending For The Faith:**

Faith manifestation is in the market place not in the church. There is no faith to contend in the church. I believe that even the enemy recognized Sunday morning to keep away from those that goes to church, allow them finish their service and house fellowship. Then on Monday issues of life will began to manifest, when the faith that you have received on Sunday is required to be put in practice.

Contending for the faith is not a onetime event. It is a continuous lifestyle of every Christian to contend for the faith in the house, in the office, in the neigbourhood, in the place of work or business arena.

In Dan. 3:14-16 "Nebuchadnezzar spake and said unto them, is it true, O Shadrach, Meshach and Abed-nego, do not ye serve my gods, nor worship the golden image which I have set up? Now if ye be ready that at what time ye hear the sound of the cornet, flute, harp, sackbut, psaltery, and dulcimer, and all kinds of musick, ye fall down and worship the image which I have made, well but if ye worship not, ye shall be cast the same hour into the midst of a burning fiery furnace, and who is that God that shall deliver you out of my hands? Shadrach, Meshach and abed0nego answered and said to the king, O Nebuchadnezzar, we are not careful to answer thee in this matter".

Contending for the faith is not what any believer goes about looking for faith to contend with. The issue of contending for the faith comes naturally to every believer.

As an apostle in the market place, it is not in your hand to decide the kind of things that will come your way to contend for the faith. But it is required that as you live your life or work in an office there are issues that will want you to compromise your faith when those events come in the office, in the market place, in the neighbourhood, in your family, remember that we are surrounded with many witnesses that want to see your reaction to it. The bible said in Heb. 12:1 "wherefore seeing we also are compassed about with so great a cloud of witnesses let us lay aside every weight, and the sin which doth so easily beset us, and let us run so easily beset us, and let us run with patience the race that is set before us".

There is a race set before every believer everyday of life. You cannot shift the responsibility to another person neither would you not run your own race because all those around that knows that you are a believer is watching you.

Victory comes after contention. The three Hebrew children became what they were because they refuse to compromise; they prefer to fear God than to fear a king. The result of their contending for the faith was God's name be glorified in Dan. 3:28 "Then Nebuchadnezzar spake, and said blessed be the God of Shadrach, Meshach and Abed-nego, who hath sent his angel, and delivered his servants that trusted in him, and have changed the king's word, and yielded their bodies, that they might not serve nor worship any other god except their own God".

In Dan. 3:29 "There I make a decree that every people, nation and language, which speak anything amiss against the God of Shadrach, Meshach and Abed-nego, shall be cut in piece, and their houses shall be made a dunghill <u>because there is no other God that can deliver after this sort</u>.

The end product of contending for the faith is to bring the glory of God to bear in the life of people or nation.

God need to be glorified in the lives of people around us, this can only take place depending upon our attitude to issues that come our way.

Every apostle in market place must prepare constantly to contend for the faith in the market place. It is part of the growth and glory of the apostle in the market place.

When issues to contend for our faith comes, it does not ring bell. You may not understand it that way but that event may make or mar your destiny all depends upon your response to it.

In the case of Daniel after the interpretation of dream it appears he is now comfortable but contending for the faith is a continuous act.

You don't tell God when to test you neither will you tell the enemy to stop issues that requires you to contend for the faith

Only be prepared to arise and defend the faith that you profess like Daniel in Dan. 6:10 "Now when Daniel knew that the writing was signed, he went into his house, and his windows being open in his chamber toward Jerusalem, he kneeled upon his knees three time a day, and prayed, and gave thanks before his God as he did aforetime".

Daniel saw the need to contend for his faith irrespective of the decree of the king.

He saw the move as a direct challenge to his faith. It was issue between his life, his position and his faith. He decided to contend for his faith. I believe he must have said the same thing Esther said in the book of Esther 4:16 "Go gather together all the Jews that are present in Shushan, and fast ye for me and neither neither eat nor drink three days night or day. I also and my maidens will fast likewise, and so will I go in with the king, which is not according to the law and <u>if I perish, I perish</u>".

As apostle in the market place you are expected like Daniel, Esther etc to contend for the faith you believe. The contention of your faith may be as regards your position in the place of your work; it may be your Christianity, marriage even sometimes in the area of your children.

What is demanded from us is to contend for the faith because we are surrounded with cloud of witnesses watching us.

The resultant effect of contending for the faith by apostles in the market place are:

Firstly God is glorified in Daniel 6:26 – 27 "I make a decree, that in every dominion of my kingdom men tremble and fear before the |God of Daniel, for he is the living God, and steadfast forever, and his kingdom that which shall not be destroyed and his dominion shall be even unto the end. He delivereth and rescureth and he worked signs and wonders in heaven and in earth, who hath delivered Daniel from the power of the Lions."

Secondly the apostle in the market place God prospers him or her as seen in Daniel 6:28" So this Daniel prospered in the reign of Danius and in the reign of cyrus the Persian"

Thirdly other apostles in the market place are encouraged to contend for their own faith.

Fourthly most often it leads to salvation of the Gentiles or unbelievers or rededication of life of those Christians that have backslidden.

h. **Encouragement:**

This is a natural function of an apostle in the market place. You discovered that the moment your colleague in the place of work or neighbourhood noticed that you are a committed believer, once he or she has a problem looking for people to encourage him, they look for apostles in the market place to encourage them or pray with them.

Prayer partners of most workers or people you found in the market place are apostles in the market place. The reason is that they see somebody who share the same challenges they are facing and need somebody who will encourage them and pray for them

As a lawyer most often I have gone beyond legal advice to spiritual advice to my clients, several times I have ended up praying for such client that came for legal advice. Your colleague, professional partners who see how God is blessing you or helping you in your business comes to you for encouragement or prayers.

Paul was one of the greatest apostles of our Lord that lived here on earth.

But Paul wouldn't have been what he is today if not the important roles two men played in his conversion and ministry.

The first person is a relatively unknown disciple called Ananias who responded to the demand of God to visit Paul and pray for him, in Acts 9:17 – 19 "And Ananias went his way and entered into the house and putting his hands on him said, brother Saul, the Lord, even Jesus, That appeared unto there in the way as thou camest, hath sent me, that thou mightiest receive thy sight, and be filled with the Holy Ghost. And immediately there fill from his eyes as it had been scales, and he received sight forth with, and arose, and was baptized. And when he had received meat, he was strengthened. Then was Saul contain days with the disciples which were at Damascus".

The second person that played important role in the ministry of Paul is Barnabas called the son of encouragement in Acts 9:27 "But Barnabas took him, and brought him to the apostles and declared unto them how he had seen the Lord in the way, and that he had spoken to him, and how he had preached boldly at Damascus in the name of Jesus".

The results of what Ananias and Barnabas did to Paul can be seen in Act 9:28 – 29 "And he was with the coming in and going out at Jerusalem. And he spake boldly in the name of the Lord Jesus, and disputed against the Grecians: but they went about to slay him".

In the market place we the apostles have a great opportunity to minister to people whom bring their challenges for us to pray with them or encourage them.

As apostles in the market place, we should utilize every opportunity that called for our counseling or praying to lead the person to Christ if that person is not a believer.

It is our duties to be prepared every time to give encouragement or prayers to a hurting heart in 2Tim. 4:2 preach the word, be instant in season out of season, reprove, rebuke, exhort with all long suffering and doctrine".

There are various functions or assignment God gives out to the apostles in the market place but the end result of all of them is to save life and manifest the glory of God.

CHAPTER FOUR

WHAT IS LIGHT?

Light was defined by Merrian –webster as "Something that makes vision possible". Light is something that illuminates. It is easier to find something when there is a light. People grope in darkness, the movement of people are slowed down once there is darkness.

We know that darkness is the opposite of light. Seeing darkness helps us to understand light and the benefits thereof.

Light came into existence by God. God understand light and knows the importance of light to humanity and the entire world.

In *Genesis 1:3,5* "And God said let there be light and there was light... 5 "And God called the light day and the darkness he called night. And the evening and the morning were the first day".

In *Genesis 1:14 – 18* "And God said, let there be light in the firmament of the heaven to divide the day from the night, and let them be for signs and for seasons, and for days and years. And let them be for light in the firmament of the heaven to give light upon the earth. And it was so and God made two great lights, the greater light to rule the day, and the lesser light to rule the night. He made the stars also. And God set them in the firmament of the heaven to give light upon the earth and to rule over the day and over the night, and to divide the light form the darkness, and God saw that it was good".

When God created the light He had reason why He created it to. From the day light was created till date, it has not failed to carry out its function as assigned by God. Looking at *Genesis 1:14-18* we could see some of the functions of light as follows:
1. The light was created to divide the day from the night. In other words light is a separator. It can separate you or anything so that their importance can be seen or realized.

In separating the day from the night it tries to define to humanity the kind of function that can be carried out in the day and the one that can be done in the night.

2. The light is meant to be for signs and seasons and for days and years. This has helped us to define days, weeks, months and years. It has helped humanity to know what to expect in terms of season.
3. It is meant to give light to the earth. It does not allow the continuance dominant of darkness over the earth. So it regulate the activities of man. Man now knows that major activities are done during the day, while there is light and lesser activities during the night.
4. The light is to rule over the earth the greater light rules the day, while the lesser light rules the night. If when God created the light He assigned this great responsibility to the light and now as market place apostle, Jesus said we are the light of the world.

We can say that God referring us as light had the same function He assigned to light to us. He except us to fulfill the same function as was given to light. The good news is that from the date of creation till date light has been carrying out this function without failure.

It means that our life needs to show to the world the difference between good and evil, because we are meant to be a separator between good and evil. This can be realized in the lifestyle we live and things we do for the kingdom of God.

Secondly as light is meant to be for signs, we are expected to be for signs and wonders in *Mark 15:15-17* "And he said unto them go ye into all the world and preach the gospel to every creature. He that believeth and is baptized shall be saved, but he that believeth not shall be dammed. And these signs shall follow them that believe in my name shall they cast out devils, they shall speak with now tongues".

Every market place apostle that operate in this spiritual realm is said to be for signs and wonders to his generation. God expect us to get involved in His kingdom purpose and He has promised us that these signs shall follow us.

God did not say these signs shall follow the pastors or general overseer of churches or president of fellowships but shall follow those that believe.

Simple belief in what God had promised us ensures that signs follow our belief and our functions in the kingdom of God.

As market place apostle if signs are not following you, check if your lifestyle or functions is in line with God directives in the bible. So be the light that God wants you to be and become a sign to your family, your nation and your generation.

Part of it function is to give light to the earth, as a market place apostle you are expected to give light to the earth. It means that you will not allow the continues dominant of darkness over the earth. Every act of darkness on earth must be resisted by your activities in the market place. Where you refused to shine as light you are encouraging darkness to dominate.

Some apostles in the market place had relocated from one house to another because of fear of a witch or occultic people. It ought not to be so. If you are being oppressed by darkness or your neighbourhood by darkness, it means you are not shinning enough to eschew darkness from your vicinity.

God ordained the great light to rule by day while lesser light rule by night. So God assigned function to light is to rule either by day or night.

It is in recognition of this function that the psalmists wrote in ***Psalm 121:6*** "the sun shall not smite thee by day, nor the moon by night".

It is in recognition of the function of light in ruling by day or night that the psalmist addressed the source of light working against him.

When we relate this function to an apostle of the market place we realize that we as light of the world are expected to rule over darkness both in the day or night.

Jesus said in ***Matthew 16:19*** "And I will give unto thee the key of heaven and whatsoever thou shall bind on earth shall be bound in heaven and whatsoever thou shall loose on earth shall be loosed in heaven". Jesus repeated this in ***Matthew 18:18*** "Verily I say unto you whatsoever ye shall bind on earth shall be bound in heaven and whatsoever ye shall loose on earth shall be loosed in heaven".

The responsibility of controlling both the day and the night has been assigned by God to all believers. It means that you have been ordained by God to control the spiritual that control the physical. It is only those things you permit to happen in your life, family or nation that will happen whether in the day or in the night. God said you are the light of the world means God had given us the right and authority to be in control of things around us. This authority is permissible when you are in covenant relationship with God, this is also in line with God's original plan for man in ***Genesis 1:28*** "And God blessed them and God said unto them be fruitful and multiply and replenish the earth and subdue it and have dominion over the fish of the sea and over the fowl of the air and over everything that moveth upon the earth".

Another thing we need to know about light is as stated in ***Genesis 1:4*** "And God saw the light that it was good and God divided the light from the darkness".

As light, God sees you as good. It does not matter how the world sees you. It does not matter how your family and those around you see you now but God's proclamation of you is good. So it is expected that you should manifest goodness all around you. It also means that no matter what circumstances is now the end product of what God had put in you is goodness.

If God's expectation of you as a light is goodness, you are not expected to be involved with anything that is not good in the eyes of God. There must be goodness in your life, marriage, health and finances. Believe that as light there is nothing in you or around you that is not good. Everything in you is good and must manifest God's goodness.

In the same scripture we read in *Genesis 1:4* we were informed that God divided the light from darkness. God separated the light from darkness. Light is meant to be separated from darkness. Light has nothing in common with darkness and do not have the potency to comprehend light. Light is on a class of its own. There is no comparison between light and darkness. darkness does not exist where light dwells. Light has the potential of over shadowing darkness whenever it comes in contact with it.

From the beginning God separated us as light from darkness. God expect us to live as light and not to be associated with darkness.

In *2Corinthians 6:14* "Be ye not unequally yoked together with unbelievers. For what fellowship hath righteousness with unrighteousness? And what communion hath light with darkness".

There is no fellowship or communion between light and darkness. The presence of light is the disappearance of darkness and the presence of darkness put light in a abeyance.

There is no combination between light and darkness you cannot be partial light and partial darkness. It is either you are light or you are darkness.

It is for you to decide whether to be light or to be darkness. But don't pretend to be light and manifest in darkness. It does not work.

The bible said in *Ephesians. 5:8* "For ye were sometimes darkness, but now are ye light in the Lord; walk as children of light".

If you have become light do not continue to manifest in darkness that you were manifesting before you became light.

You were once darkness before you gave your life to Jesus Christ and thereafter became light, so every past lifestyle of darkness must be dropped for you to enjoy the glorious benefit of being light.

In *1Thesselonians 5:5* "Ye are all the children of light, and the children of the day. We are not of the night nor of darkness".

Do not manifest what you are not. A human being behaves like such and do not behave like a Gorilla or monkey. We must always remember that we are children of light not of the night nor of darkness.

Today we are admonished by the bible how we manifest the light which we are see *Luke 11:35* "Take heed therefore that the light which is in thee be not darkness".

When you are light and you refused to manifest as light it is tantamount to darkness. People around you are expected to benefit from your light and when people are not benefiting from your light it can only be likened that your light has become darkness.

As light God expectation of us is captioned in *Luke 1:79* "To give light to them that sit in darkness and in the shadow of death to guide our feet into the way of peace".

There is expectation in every corner, people are waiting to see leaders that will be light to them. Families are waiting for men and women that will be unto them and show them the way of peace.

As a market place apostle can people around you say indeed they have seen light in you as in *Matthew 4:16* "The people which sat in darkness saw great light, and to them which sat in the region and shadow of death light is spring up".

All over the world people are waiting for the manifestation of light. Those who could not access light through Jesus Christ had ended up in wrong religion or cultism in a bid to seek for light. All the men or women you found in these wrong religion or cultism, their primary pursuit was for light that will guarantee them power. They have an understanding that light always prevail over darkness and in a bid to get this light have been deceived by the devil pretending as angel of light. In *2Corinthians 11:14* "And no marvel, for satan himself is transformed unto an angel of light".

Devil cannot be light, he is nothing but darkness. In order to deceive he tries to transform himself into an angel of light but he is not light and nothing good is in him or in his darkness.

You cannot obtain benefit by a little darkness around it. Every presence of darkness near the light reduces the level of shinning of the light,the brightness of light during day time is greater than the brightness of light during the night.

Darkness does not have dominion over light expect a covenant time allowed by God for darkness to manifest and which is only in the night. There is no other time darkness is permitted to occupy a space in time. Even in the covenant time of darkness during night, light still has dominance once natural and generated light comes up darkness surely disappears.

The preeminence of light over darkness cannot be over emphasized. The creator of light and darkness from the beginning gave light an uncontroverted dominance over darkness. God made the dominance of light over darkness as a non contentious issue. Light does not struggle or fight to have dominance over darkness. In other hand if we the apostles of the market place manifest as light over the earth, our dominance over evil darkness and it's cohort shall not be a thing of struggle or exertion of strength.

If our life manifest light wherever we work or live our dominance over darkness within our environment becomes a natural thing without undue conflict or struggle.

Darkness from immemorial till date have never contended over the dominance of light over it, so no darkness have the power to contend over us when we manifest as light.

Light is not afraid of darkness so any time you become fearful, it is either you are not a light or you lack knowledge of who you are in Christ Jesus.

Light does not negotiate with darkness or goes into peace talk with darkness. So every compromise in the life of a believer, an apostle in the market place is nothing but an act of going into peace talk with darkness.

But know that darkness does not hold peace talk because it does not release his prisoners. In *Isaiah 14:12-17* "How art thou fallen from heaven, O Lucifer, son of the morning! How art thou cut down to the ground, which didst weaken the nations. For thou last said in thine heart, I will ascend into heaven, I will exalt my throne above the stars of God, I will sit also upon the mount of the congregation, in the sides of the north, I will ascend above the heights of the clouds, I will be like the most High. Yet thou shalt be brought down to hell, to the sides of the pit. They that see thee shall narrowly look upon thee, and consider thee saying, is this man that made the earth to tremble, that did share kingdoms that made the world as a wilderness **and destroyed the cities thereof; that opened not the house of his prisoners?**

God did not ordain that light should go into negotiation or compromise with darkness but only to have dominion without negotiation or compromise.

We as light is also ordained by God to have dominion over everything on earth including darkness as God declared it *Genesis 1:28* "And God blessed them, and God said unto them, be fruitful and multiply, and replenish the earth, and subdue it, and have dominion over the fish of the sea, and over the fowl of the air, and over every living thing that moveth upon the earth".

Let us stop complaining about the activities of darkness around us but keep on shinning, as we shine, darkness will have no other option than to give way.

CHAPTER FIVE

WHAT THE WORLD REPRESENT

The world is a geographical area inhabited by human beings. The world has so many activities going on from the day of creation till when rapture will take place.

In john 17:11-12 "And now I am no more in the world, but these are in the world … while I was with them in the world, I kept them in thy name…"

Jesus in the above statement informed us that the world is a place of habitation. It was in the world that Jesus lived and performed his miracles. It was in the world He raised disciples that He trained and those apostles/disciples lived here in the world after Jesus had gone.

When Jesus came he did not go to the mars, venus, moon or other planets, he came to the world where people dwell as we can see in Ps. 24:1 "The earth is the Lord's and the fullness thereof, the world, and they that dwell therein". The world is a dwelling place for people. In Ps. 33:8 "Let all the earth fear the Lord, Let all the inhabitant of the world stand in awe of him".

Also in Ps. 49:1 "Hear this all ye people give ear, all ye inhabitants of the world. From the foregoing it is an established fact that the world is a place of habitation for people and other God's creatures.

The world is full of different races, tribe, nations and kindred inhabiting one part or the other. It is also permitted that you can migrate from your place of habitation to another part of the world to dwell.

The world has men that dwell in it and referred to as men of the world See Ps. 17:14 "From men which are thy hand, O Lord from men of the world which have their portion in this life and whose belly thou fullest with thy hid treasure they are full of children and leave the rest of their substance to their babes."

The world accommodates men that will dwell in it and the children and grand children (babes) of these men also inhabit this world. So the world is primarily a place of habitation for men and their family.

Taking a look at the above mentioned scripture you will discover that the substance of the men which they enjoy and leave as an inheritance to their children and grand children is in the same world.

This goes to underscore the importance of the world to men and their family; it also means that any spiritual being like God will be interested in the world. Equally the interest of God in this world attract the devil to work against God's interest in the world.

It is important to note that though the world is a place of habitation for man and his family and his substance but it was not created by man. God is the creator of this world, He lays the foundation of the world in Ps. 50:12 "If I were hungry, I would not tell thee, for the world is mine and the fullness thereof".

God asserted that the world belongs to him and planted man He created to dwell therein with all the fullness God prepared and kept for man in this world. God has love for the world He created and even has an agenda for the world. In John 3:16 "For God so loved the world, that He gave His only begotten son, that whosoever believeth in him should not perish not have everlasting life".

The love of God for the world He created attracts God's enemy and it worked against God interest through man.

In Isa. 14:17 "That made the world as a wilderness and destroyed the cities thereof, that opened not the house of his prisoners".

The love of God for the world attracted the devil's envy, hatred and anger against the world and the people thereof these attack by the devil has made the world not to be exactly what God intended the world to be.

We shall examine various acts or events that have taken place in the world as a result of this nefarious act of the devil against the world. The enemy succeeded in creating rebellious kingdom in the world that opposes the agenda of God in Matt. 4:8 "Again, the devil taketh him up into an exceeding high mountain, and sheweth him all the kingdoms of the world and the glory of them".

Today these various kingdoms known as occult groups have led the men of the world astray from serving that true God. These kingdoms in the world have risen to oppose everything that promotes God's agenda in the world.

The decent of the glory of these kingdoms have attracted so many men and led them astray. It was the same attraction the devil was showing Jesus to cause him to deviate from God given agenda. Today many men that have followed the attractions of these kingdoms in the world have mortgaged their soul and eternal life and have missed their God given destiny.

The rise of these kingdoms in the world today have been on the increase without an equal rise from the men of the world that is allegiance to God's purpose and agenda.

The attractions of these deceitful glories of these kingdoms have made some men of the world to follow occultic practices or false religion just to satisfy the lust of the eyes, the lust of the flesh or the pride of life.

These kingdom activities of the devil had led so many astray and led to various and led cares of the world. Many have been entangled with the cares of the world resulting from the acts of the enemy of the men of the world.

In Mark 4:19 "And the cares of this world, and the deceitfulness of riches and lusts of the other things entering in choke the world and it becometh unfruitful".

Part of the challenges men who live in the world are the cares of the world. These cares of the world arose as a result of the fall of Adam in the Garden of Eden. When God created man he placed here in the world God provided all that man needed see Gen. 28,9 " The Lord God planted eastward on Eden and there he put the man whom he had formed. And out of the ground the Lord God made every tree grow that pleasant to the sight and good for food".

Because of the fall of Adam, he was driven out of the Garden of Eden into the world. Gen. 3:22 -24 "Then the Lord God said Behold the man has become like one of us to know good and evil. And now lest he put out his hand and take also of the tree of life, and eat and live forever. Therefore the Lord God sent him out of the Garden of Eden to till the ground from which he was taken. So he drove out the man and He placed Cherubim at the east of the Garden of Eden".

The fall of Adam drove him into the world to face the cares of the world and generation after Adam had continued in this toils and cares of the world.

When Jesus came he knew that part of the problem facing the inhabitants of the world is the cares of the world. He realized that the act of men most often is influenced by the cares of the world.

He also realized that the cares of the world had limited the time of service and fellowship men ought to have with God.

The care of this world is capable of choking men and pushing them out of their divine destiny and Jesus offered help in Matt. 11:28-30 "Come to me, all you who labour and are heavy laden and I will give you rest. Take my yoke upon you and learn from me, for I am gentle and lowly in heart and you will find rest for your souls. For my yoke is easy and my burden is light"

If we the inhabitants of the world can drop the cares of the world and come to Jesus, definitely He will give us rest and even our soul shall find rest in him.

Though there is a yoke and burden to carry when you follow Jesus. But He said his yoke and burden is light compared to the cares of the world.

Jesus went further to admmish the men of the world to forgo the cares of the world and seek God and His righteousness in Matt. 6:31-33 "therefore do not worry saying what shall we eat? Or what shall we drink? Or what shall we wear? For after all these things the Gentiles seek. For your heavenly father knows that you need them all these things. But seek first the kingdom of God and His righteousness and all these things shall be added to you".

Though there are cares in the world Jesus is the cure or solution to the cares of the world. It then means that we who are the apostles at the market place that are confronted with the cares of the world on daily basis ought to be the agent of that solution to humanity.

In our field of endeavours we have wonderful testimonies of how we gave our lives to Jesus and God intervened in the cares around us and granted peace, rest and personal fulfillment in our desires.

The only way any man can avoid the cares of the world and still have peace, rest and fulfillment of desires is by giving his life to Jesus and becoming instrument in the hand of God to point others to Jesus for their personal solution.

The world today is full with people who are hurting because of the cares of the world, who don't have an understanding of how they can overcome the cares of the world choking life out of them. He who sows the good seed is the son of man. The world we know is a field see Matt. 13:27-43 "The field is the world, the good seeds are the sons of the kingdom, but the tares are the sons of the wicked one. The enemy who sowed them is the devil, the harvest is the end of the age and the reapers are the angels. Therefore as the tares are gathered and burned in the fire, so it will be at the end of the age.

The son of man will send out His kingdom all they will gather out of His kingdom all things that offend and those who practice lawlessness and will cast them into the furnace of fire. There will be wailing and garnishing of teeth. Then the righteous will shine forth as the son in the kingdom of the father".

Because the world is a field there is need to xray the scripture mentioned above. That scripture brought out to bare that as it is in a field so it is in the world that God (son of man), man, angels and the devil are all involved.

Apart from personalities involved seed, tares and ground of the world are also involved. We need to look at different functions or activities mentioned in relation to the world.

The world is where both good and bad seed are sown. The scripture we read said Jesus sows the good seed which he was referred to as son of man. Today Jesus is not physically present but have left the responsibility of sowing good seed in the hands of sons of man, we the apostles at the market place.

When Jesus was in the world he took the responsibilities of sowing good seed everywhere in Acts 10:38 "How God anointed Jesus of Nazareth with the Holy Ghost and with power who went about doing good, good and healing all that were oppressed of the devil, for God was with him. Jesus has left an example for us as market place apostles to follow.

Going by the bible verse of Acts 10:38 it means that all of us who have been anointed by God through the Holy Spirit must move from one place to the other in this world doing good and planting good seed in the lives of people.

Part of our function in this world as market place apostles is to engage in healing all that were oppressed of the devil. The anointing we have is not for show, it is for sowing good seed as Jesus had left example for us. If we look at the act of Jesus in the bible his work was done primarily in the market place except few he did in the synagogue.

For every opportunity we have here in this world as sons of men and the market place apostles is to sow good seed and involve in doing good and healing all those that are been oppressed by the devil.

Look around you now, you will see colleagues, neighbours and family members that are hurting or oppressed by the devil in the area of their marriage perhaps thinking or planning divorce, there are some in a terrible financial problems caused by the oppression of the devil, some in serious health problems or children's rebellion they are all caused by the oppression of the devil.

Part of sowing the good seed is by praying for them until they are saved or healed or delivered from the oppression of the enemy. Whereby encouraging the prevalence over darkness or activities of the devil.

Every day of your life, you are either involved in sowing god seed or bad seed as you carry your daily activities. You are going about everyday of your work or existence either sowing good seed or encouraging bad seed to be sown by your act of indifference.

The anointing we have received is not just to speak in tongues alone or prophesy, we must engage the power of God in sowing good seed. Be reminded what the bible said in Eccl. 12:1, 6, 7 "Remember now thy creator in the days of thy youth, while the evil days come not, nor the years draw nigh, when thou shalt say, I have no pleasure in them". Or ever the silver cord be loosed, or the golden bowl be broken or the pitcher be broken at the fountain or the wheel broken at the cistern. Then shall the dust return to the earth as it was and the spirit shall return unto God who gave it".

Remember we have a limited time to stay here in the world before we return back to heaven, so we have to do all we can to sow good seed while breath is still in us.

Since part of the reason God created the world is for sowing seed, we should endeavour to follow the steps of Jesus as we go about doing our work or business, we should engage in the act of sowing good seed here in the world.

The sowing of the good seed and activities of tares in the world are activities that are going on in simultaneously, the preponderance of one is dependent of whether those who are sowing good seed are more in number than those sowing tares.

Failure to sow any of them becomes an encouragement for the sowing of the other that is to say if those who are sowing good seed are more in number than those who are sowing tares good will prevail in the world.

That evil is in the increase in the world is an attestation that only few are sowing good seed. The only way we can decrease the activities of evil is in the sowing of good seed.

The activities of the tares sown by sons of the wicked ones can be seen manifesting everywhere. Peace has become a precious product in the world today as a result of the activities of sowing tares by the sons of the wicked ones. Violence, the imagination of men are ready to increase if it is not tamed by sowing good seed by the sons of men here in the world. Jesus had done His own part and left the continuation of sowing good seeds in the world in our hands. If we fail to sow good seeds in the world we should not blame God for the increase of the activities of sowing tares by the sons of the wicked ones.

Because the world is a field as the bible had informed us. It is important to note that in this field devil is also involved. So if you have a personal field or farm and you know the devil or enemy is interested in your field or farm, it beholds on you to do all that is necessary to protect your product in the field, you will also endeavour to sow good seeds in every part of the field or farm to avoid tares growing on any part of the field.

Because if you allow tares to grow on your field or farm, it cost you time and man power to remove the tares and if you decide to ignored the tares in your field, you are sure that your good seeds you sow may not produce quality harvest or the tares may sometimes choked the good seed to death or to minimal harvest.

The reason a farmer weeds his farm constantly is to avoid tares taking over his farm or destroying his good seeds.

This field called the world is a field the devil entered before the sons of man and has an agenda to frustrate the destiny of the sons of man which we can see in Gen 3:1, 4 "Now the serpent was more subtle than any beast of the field which the Lord God had made. And he said unto the woman, yea hath God said, ye shall not eat of every tree of the garden. And the serpent said unto the woman ye shall not surely die".

That after the initial act of devil sowing tares in the lives of Adam and Eve, it has not stopped the act of sowing tares in the lives of men and women of the world.

The devil tries to sow tares in the life of Jesus see Matt. 4:1 "Then was Jesus led up of the spirit into the wilderness to be tempted of the devil". In Matt. 4:3 And when the tempter came to him, he said if thou be the son of God command these stones be made bread".

Thank God that Jesus did not give the devil opportunity to sow tares in his life or ministry. It means that every personnel in this world can be affected by the devil sowing tares in him or his ministry.

Today the devil has known the act of sowing tares in the lives of people in the world. It is only when you are able to stop the devil from sowing tares in your life that you can be empowered to deliver those whom the devil has sown tares in their life.

It was after Jesus stopped the devil from sowing tares in his life and ministry that He returned from the wilderness in power of the Holy Ghost see Luke 4:14 "And Jesus returned in the power of the spirit into Galilee and there went out a fame of him through all the region, roundabout".

The victory Jesus had over devil empowered him to deliver those whom devil succeeded in sowing tares in their lives as stated in Acts 10:38 "… healing all that were oppressed of the devil, for God was with him".

The devil has not stopped the act of sowing tares in the lives of people up till now that is why the world is waiting for the manifestation of the sons of men that will deliver those oppressed by the devil see Rom. 8:19 – 21 "for the earnest expectation of the creature waiteth for the manifestation of the sons of God. For the creature was made subject to vanity, not willingly, but by reason of him who hath subjected the same in hope. Because the creature itself also shall be delivered from the bondage of corruption into the glorious liberty of the children of God".

If we realize the fact that in this field called the world, devil is in with great determination to sow tares in everybody whom it comes in contact with, then we should double our effort to increase the act of sowing good seeds. The enemy, the devil knows his time is short and recruited more men to continue the act of sowing tares in the lives of men. See Rev. 12:9 - 12 "And the great dragon was cast that old serpent called the devil and Satan, which <u>deceiveth the whole world: he was cast out into the earth and his angels were cast out with him</u>... Therefore rejoice ye heavens, and ye that dwell in them. Woe to the inhabitants of the earth and of the Sea: for the devil is come down unto you having great wrath, because he knoweth that he hath but a short time".

In this world there will be a time of harvest and that time is when God wil send His Son to rapture those that received Jesus as stated in John 1:12.

The bible said that God will send His angels who will come to this field to gather the harvest for God. The Angel will gather the good seeds for the Lord and those bad seeds will be gathered and thrown into the lake of fire as we were informed in Matt. 13:37 – 43.

If we have been informed by the Bible that there is going to be harvest time in the world we live in, it behoves on us to be agent of reconciliation to people around us as apostles in the market place. The danger of allowing our siblings, neighbors, colleagues to go to hell is grievous that we cannot allow our loved ones or neighbors to test it.

The world we live in shall be judged and punished for their evil deeds see Ps. 98:9 "Before the Lord; for he cometh to judge the world, and the people with equity". And in Isa. 13:11 "And I will punish the world for their evil and the wicked for their iniquity, and I will cause the arrogancy of the proud to cease, and will lay low the haughtiness of the terrible".

The world is expected to come to an end see Matt. 13:49 "As therefore the tares are gathered and burned in the fire, so shall it be in the end of this world. So shall it be at the end of the world: The angels shall come forth, and sever the wicked from among the just."

The world we live in has been programmed by God to come to an end. Unfortunately none of us knows when this end will come.

But the Bible has given us an indication when we shall see the signs of the end of the world see Matt. 24:3 "And as he sat upon the mount of Olives, he disciples came unto him privately, saying, tell us, when shall these things be and what shall be the sign of thy coming and the end of the world".

If you take a look at what Jesus answered in response to the above question in Matt. 24:4 – 41 you will agree with me that the signs of the end time of this world are already here with us. This should compel us as apostles in the market place to engage more in the work of the kingdom before the world will come to an end, when there will be no more opportunity to sow good seeds in the lives of people in the world.

Matt. 24 made us to understand that there will be tribulation in the world before it comes to an end. Various events shall herald the coming to an end of the world.

Another characteristics of the world we are referring to in this book is the act of marrying as stated in Luke 20:34 "And Jesus answering said unto them, the children of this world marry and are given in marriage".This is the known activities we witness on the world but it should not stand to distract us from the purpose of our life here in the world. Our major focus in life here is to be involved in reconciling the world to her maker and those that dwell thereof.

2 Cor. 5:18-19 "And all things are of God who hath reconciled us to himself by Jesus Christ and hath given to us the ministry of reconciliation. To wit that God was in Christ, reconciling their trespass unto them and hath committed unto us the word of reconciliation".

To help us to do this work of reconciliation for God in this world, it is pertinent to note that the dwellers in this world do not know Jesus see John 1:10 "He was in the world and the world was made by him and the world knew him not".

Because the inhabitants of the world do not know Jesus, evil increased, iniquities and wickedness became the order of the day in the world. The bible described the situation of the world then in 1 John 5;19 "And we know that we are of God and the whole world lieth in wickedness".

Because the world lieth in wickedness we should learn to be proactive in our sowing good seeds in the world. We should not allow the wickedness seen in the world to affect our responsibilities to the dying world.

May be we have done good to people in the past perhaps they have returned it back to us with evil, still don't get discouraged because what you are seeing is the manifestation of wickedness going on in the world.

The more we see manifestation of wickedness in the world the more we should go all out plant good seeds for the purpose of God's kingdom.

Today you can bear witness that stories abound of all kind of wickedness perpetrated by parents to children, siblings to their fellow sibling's, children to their parents, neighbours to other neighours, these are all acts to prove that the world lieth in wickedness.

The same bible said darkness cannot comprehend light and cannot rule over light. So as apostles in the market place, the light of the world, our activities should exhibit light that will overshadow the activities of darkness.

When you see this act of wickedness done in the world including massive killings of people it is only to remind you that you are in the world to propagate his kingdom. For everybody that comes into the world there is a time of departure from the world in John 13:1 "Now before the feast of the Passover, when Jesus know that his hour has come that he should depart out of this world into the father, having loved his own which were in the world, he loved them unto the end".

As there was a time of entrance for Jesus into the world so there was also a time of departure from the world. So many people born into the world have a date set apart for his or her departure from the world. The only unfortunate thing about departure is that most often you don't know the time or date it will occur. It is easier to predict the entrance of a person in the world than to predict departure of a person from the world.

Since we have known that there is always a time for everyone in this world to depart, it is important to us to realize that we have a date with destiny to depart this world. This should encourage to speedy up our soul winning programmes Eccl. 12:1, 5 "Remember now thy creator in the days of thy youth, while the evil days come not, nor the years draw nigh , when thou shalt say I have no pleasure in them. Also when they shall be afraid of that which is high and fears shall be in the way, the way and the almond tree shall flourish and the grasshopper shall be a burden and desire shall fail, because man goeth to his long home and the mourners go about the street".

We are informed that we can be taken out of the world see John 17:15 "I pray not that thou shouldest take them out of the world, but that thou shouldest keep them from the evil".

In the same John 17:18 "As thou hast sent me into the world even so have I also sent then into the world".

Jesus is telling all apostles in the market place that as God sent Jesus into the world that is how Jesus had sent us into the world.

Let us know that we are not in the world by accident or by the will or agreement of our parents. It is God that through Jesus sent us into this world to be the light of the world so that the people of the world will see our good deeds and glorify God and it will become a contact point for them to embrace Christ after glorifying God. We are sent out people in the world. We are not in the world first for our personal reasons.

We are sent out people to the world to continue the work Jesus left for us when He was in the world i.e to propagate the kingdom of God.

The world sometime offers people opportunity to gain it but loose themselves or become cast away see Luke 9:25 "For what is a man advantaged, if he gains the whole world and lose himself or be cast away".

It means that one can get lost in the activities that go on in the world and eventually lose the most important thing he or she has, the soul.

The activities of the world have recently be fashioned in a way that you are deeply involved with many activities that denies you the opportunity of deep fellowship with God and soul winning had been relegated to the back ground left to the time of convenience.

Personal ambition, pursuit of wealth or career had kept some of us in bondage and that time to pursue God's kingdom agenda is relegated to the background.

As apostles in the market place, this is the time to wake up the calling of God in us and pursue God's agenda before we are taking out of the world. Age or righteousness is no longer the determinant factor of when you could be taken out of the world. It is important to make haste while the sun shines.

We need to realize that duration of our stay in this world is not in our hand as God gives us life we should endeavour to be the light of the world as apostles of market place .

Despite the fact that the world lieth in wickedness, God still love the world to save it John 3:16 For God so loved the world, that he gave his only begotten son, that whosoever believeth in him should not perish".

The love of God for the world is so much that God sent Jesus to come and die for the sins of everyone in the world so that whosoever believe in the death and resurrection of Jesus will have eternal life.

Before Jesus left the world he gave us an assignment to preach the gospel of the kingdom in all the world see Matt. 24:14 "And this gospel of the kingdom shall be preached in all the world for a witness unto all nations and then shall the end come".

RELATIONSHIP BETWEEN THE WORLD AND LIGHT
There also exist a relationship between the world and the light in John 3:19-21 "And this is the condemnation that light is come into the world and men loved darkness rather than light because their deeds were evil for every one that doeth evil hateth the light, neither cometh to the light, lest his deed should be reproved. But he that doeth truth cometh to the light that his deeds may be made manifest, that they are brought in God".

Jesus is the light that the world is enjoying John 8:12 "Then spake Jesus again unto them saying, I am the light of the world, he that followeth me shall not walk in darkness, but shall have the light of life

As you come in contact with Jesus be radiates his life in you that become the basis you also become the light of the world.

Jesus is the one that lighten everyone that comes into the world. If you refuse Jesus into your life, you cannot be light and your life will be full of darkness. See John 1:9 that was the true light, which lighten everyman that cometh into the world".

What is expected of all of us in the world is nothing but a turn to the light of the world which lighteth everyone that comes into the world. In Ps. 22:27 "all the ends of the world shall remember and turn unto the Lord and all the kindred's of the nations shall worship before thee". Since we have known what the world represent and our limited time to stay in the world, we should engage in activities that will promote the kingdom of God and turn the world upside down for God as the disciples did in Acts 17:6 "And when they found them not, they drew Jason and certain brethren unto the rulers of the city crying, these that have turned the world upside down are come hither also".

If we are prepared to turn the world upside down for the Lord like the other disciples our faith and activities will be spoken throughout the whole world.

CHAPTER SIX

THE LIGHT OF THE WORLD

We did not start as light of the world because of our past lifestyle. We were once regarded as children of the world in *Luke 16:8b* "For the children of this world ..." regarding us as children of the world was because our lifestyles were all by the detects of the world. We never have God view over things but were controlled by our world view.

This worldview attitude brought us to a lot of compromises in our job, marriage, dressing, music and every facet of life. Our life was characterized with lies, hatred, anger, envy, strife and violence.

It was this lifestyle that the scripture describe us as once been darkness *Ephesians 5:8* "For ye were sometimes darkness, but now are ye light in the Lord, walk as children of light".

From the above scripture it means that the period we were not in the Lord we were darkness. So anybody who is not in the Lord that is by giving his life to Jesus our Lord, is in darkness. Our darkness stopped when we became light in the Lord.

It is important to state that we can only be light through our Lord Jesus Christ; there is no other way for any man or woman to be light except through our Lord Jesus Christ.

From the same ***Ephesians 5:8*** we read it said now you are light. You are no longer darkness as you were before you came to the Lord Jesus Christ.

Now you are light and since you have become light the bible said in ***Ephesians 5:11*** "And have no fellowship with the unfruitful works of darkness but rather reprove them".

Since we have become light, the bible enjoins us to resist any association with darkness. Every act or works of darkness is regarded unfruitful and no person wants to embark upon an unfruitful works.

It does not matter if it appears to you that you are succeeding in any work of darkness the end result of all these work of darkness is nothing but unfruitfulness. Moreover we are encouraged not only to distance ourselves from the works of darkness but we should reprove them. We should take action to put an end to it. We should not be among those that encourage or keep silence when works of darkness is being perpetrated.

Go further to discourage acts or works of darkness and take a positive stand or act to resist every works of darkness around you. Once you notice those evil acts being done speak out or do something to discourage its continuance.

So the bible said you are the light of the world in ***Matthew 5:14*** "Ye are the light of the world. A city that is set on a hill cannot be hid".

Further in ***Acts 13:47*** "For so hath the Lord commanded us, saying, I have set thee to be a light of the Gentiles, that thou shouldest be for salvation unto the ends of the earth"

To shine as light among the gentiles is a command from God. We should adhere strictly to this command that is the gentiles are expecting and waiting for us to manifest as light to them. The gentiles are not expecting us to compromise and be like them. The reason why we as apostles in the market place are not shinning as light among the gentiles is our compromise and trying to live their lifestyle.

There is always a resulting effect to the gentiles when we manifest as light to them see *Acts 13:48* "and when the gentiles heard this, they were glad and glorified the word of the Lord and as many as were ordained to eternal life believed".

This goes to show that the eternal life of so many gentiles or unbelievers or sinners around us having been delayed or hanging as a result of our failure to manifest as light to them.

They are waiting for us to shine as light of the world for their sake and for their eternal life. Can we the apostles in the market place priorities our activities and get involved in soul winning so that the gentiles, unbelievers or sinners around us can have their eternal life guaranteed.

It is expected of us not to rest on our oars until the gentiles around us have received their salvation or they start to manifest as light in this world in *2Peter 1:19* "We also a more sure word of prophecy, whereunto ye do well that ye take heed as unto a light that shineth in a dark place, until the day dawn and the day star arise in your hearts"

Don't expect the world to be perfect before you start shinning. The bible we read said that we are to shine in dark place. Light is more appreciated when it shines in the dark. Anytime you have opportunity to view the moon when there is darkness outside, the beauty of moon becomes real.

God knew that the world we live in now by reason of the entrance of sin into it has made it to lie in wickedness. Manifestation of darkness is seen everywhere and in every facet of life.

We as apostles in the market place, it is not our duty to keep on criticizing the activities of darkness without a corresponding act to shine in the midst of darkness and also reprove the works of darkness.

What keeps darkness in abeyance is only when we shine as light, no amount of criticism, whishing can drive darkness away. It is only the entrance of light that extinguishes darkness.

If we as apostle in the market place refuses or fails to shine in the market place as light of the world, we are not justifiably to criticize any organization or government.

Stop criticizing and start shinning as light in the dark world of politics, economy, family, business etc.

Those who are walking in darkness in the world can receive light if we are ready to shine as light to them and discontinue encouraging darkness in the world. God had made provision for those that walk in darkness to receive light *Isaiah 9:2* "The people that walked in darkness have seen a great light, they that dwell in the land of the shadow of death, upon them hath the light shined".

It does not matter the level of darkness surrounding any person, the light of the world which we are can shine on such person and bring the desired change God required. Are there people around you walking by the shadow of death, your light can turn around their situation or circumstances they are facing.

We have great function as apostles in the market to deliver as many as have found themselves in the shadow of death. It is only when we manifest as light of the world that we can help them come out of the shadow of death.

Let us not allow those around us to move from the shadow of death to the real death without their eternal life secured.

Isaiah 60:1-4 "Arise, shine for thy light is come and the glory of the Lord is risen upon thee. For behold, the darkness shall cover the earth, and gross darkness the people, but the Lord shall arise upon thee, and his glory shall be seen upon thee. And the gentiles shall come to thy light and kings to the brightness of thy rising. Lift up thine eyes roundabout and see all that gather themselves together they come to thee, thy sons shall come from far and thy daughters shall be nursed at thy side."

A careful analysis of the above scripture in line with our discussion as apostles in the market place, the light of the world, the following could be deduced:

(a) If you must be the light of the world, you must arise. It is a command from the bible not a wish. To arise connotes taking a positive action. It could also mean the person had been dormant or the gifting in the person is dormant. You need to arise if you want to shine like the light of the world.

Until you arise like blind Bartimaeus you may not fulfill your destiny in **Mark 10:46 – 50** "And they came to Jericho and as he went out of Jericho with his disciples and a great number of people, blind Bartimaeus, the son of Tamaeus, sat by the highway side begging and when he heard that it was Jesus of Nazareth, he began to cry out and say Jesus thou son of David, have mercy on me. And many charged him that he should hold his peace. But he cried the more a great deal, thou son of David have mercy on me… And Jesus stood still and commanded him to be called. And they called the blind man, saying unto him, be of good comfort, rise, he calleth thee. And he casting away his garment rise and came to Jesus".

Blind Bartimaeus was on the road begging until he heard that Jesus was passing through his way and he decided to use the opportunity to change the course of his destiny.

He was dormant in the fulfillment of his destiny and when he met Jesus he was asked to arise and the bible recorded that he arose. If blind Bartimaeus did not arise, it would not have been possible for him to shine. As blind Bartimaeus came in contact with Jesus, the glory of the Lord arose on him and he began to shine because his light has come. Today he is still a reference point to a man who arose and change the course of his destiny. Until you arise, you cannot shine even if you have come in contact with the glory of the Lord.

It does not matter what you are doing now or where you are. Your story can change if only you are ready to arise and change the course of your destiny.

Your contact with the glory of God is to help you shine. God is ever ready to play his own part but you must arise, until you arise, you cannot shine

    (b) To shine means to be bright by reflection of light. It also means to cause to emit light or brightness caused by the reflection of light.

To shine is an action word attributed to sun or moon. This action carried out by the sun or moon brings out light to the world. This is a responsibility God gave to them at the beginning of creation **Genesis 1:14 – 16** "And God Said, let there be light in the firmament of the heaven to divide the day from the night, and let them be for signs, and for seasons, and for days and years. And let them be for lights in the firmament of the heaven to give light upon the earth: and it was so and God made two great lights; the greater light to rule the night he made the stars also".

From the time God assigned this responsibility to the moon and sun they have not failed God in discharging their duties both in day time and night.

When Jesus came He told us that we are the light of the world, Jesus was reminding us that as the moon and sun have not failed God we should not fail God. We should shine like the moon and the sun. It shows that the combined function of the sun and moon shines 24hours. It is also expected of us to arise and shine as the light of the world 24 hours, both in season and out of season in *2Timothy 4:2* "Preach the word; be instant in season, out of season; reprove, rebuke, exhort with all longsuffering and doctrine".

To shine as light in the world means we must be prepared to preach the word of God, we must be ready to reprove, rebuke or exhort with all longsuffering to our colleagues, neighbours and siblings. It is a responsibility God has placed upon us as apostles in the market place.

Are we prepared to please God or disappoint Him; it is left to us to decide but always remember we are the light of the world.

The moon and the sun gives the physical light to the world but the world also need the spiritual light and we are the vessel God had appointed to give that spiritual light to the world. The world is already receiving the physical light from the moon and the sun but they are waiting for our manifestation as the spiritual light of the world in **Romans. 8:19 – 21** "For the earnest expectation of the creature waiteth for the manifestation of the sons of God. For the creature was made subject to vanity, not willingly, but by reason of him who hath subjected the same in hope, because the creature itself also shall be delivered from the bondage of corruption into the glorious liberty of the children of God".

Both God and his creatures are eagerly waiting for us to manifest as light of the world.

> (c) Why must we shine, because our light has come, no man can shine on his own without the light of God. It is when a man come in contact with God's light that he can shine as light **John 1:2 – 4,9** "The same was in the beginning with God. All things were made by him and without him was not anything made that was made. In him was life, and the life was the light of men. That was the true light which lighteth every man that cometh into the world".

Jesus is the true light God sent to us to lighten every man in the world that decide to accept Jesus as that light God sent to us. Any light that the source is not from Jesus is not the true light and we need to run away from it. There is no other access to the light except by accepting Jesus into our life as our Lord and savior. No one in this world can have true light except a man or woman prepared to receive Jesus as Lord and savior.

Psalm 38:9 "For with thee is the fountain of life in thy light shall we see light". For those who crave to have light, this can only be realized through God's light. The scripture above stated it clearly that it is in the light of God that we can have light or we can see light.

For us who needs the light to overcome the darkness around us or the darkness manifesting in our business, family, marriage or spiritual life we need to receive the light that is in God Through Jesus Christ. So the fountain of life that we receive from God can properly be enjoyed when we shine as light in this world.

It is time for us to shine because our light in God that is in Christ Jesus has come, ***John 1:9*** "That was the true light, which lighteth every man that cometh into the world".

Since Jesus is the light of the world and has come into the world to die for our sins, it beholds on us to take the advantage of receiving Jesus into our lives and creating an opportunity for others to receive Jesus as Lord and savior and shines as light in the entire world.

(d) The next thing we need to consider in ***Isaiah 60:1 – 4*** that is important to our discussion is "for behold, the darkness shall cover the earth, and gross darkness the people".

God most often informs us what will take place in future through the Bible before such events happen. This is to tell us that nothing surprises God, secondly for us to be prepared before it happens, thirdly for us to concentrate on the solution to the problem rather than dwell on the problem.

God had informed us that there will be darkness and gross darkness over the earth and the people. So there is no need dissipating our energy on the darkness or activities of darkness or activities of darkness we see around us.

God is not expecting us to start been philosophical about darkness or going into debate or lectures about darkness and why the darkness.

God encountered similar things at the beginning of creation in ***Genesis 1:2*** "And the earth was without form, and void, and darkness was upon the face of the deep. And the spirit of God moved upon the face of the waters".

God left an example for us to follow. He did not get into argument with darkness or the cause of the darkness.

God simply reached out to the solution of darkness and declared it. He simply said Jesus manifest over the earth and the bible said there was light and darkness could not comprehend it.

God also expect that once we see any darkness in any facet of our lives or the lives of others all we need to do is to manifest as light.

Careful study of that *Genesis 1:2* will also tell you that though there was darkness upon the face of the deep but the spirit of God moved upon the face of the waters. It means that as God representatives whenever we see darkness fear should not limit us, we should move upon the darkness.

Once we move upon the darkness as light, definitely darkness will give way because it does not comprehend light.

What is happening in the world today as the act of darkness is not a new thing to the Lord. In *1Timothy 4:1 – 3* "Now the spirit speaketh expressly, that in the latter times some shall depart from the faith, giving heed to the seducing spirits and doctrines of devils; speaking lies and hypocrisy, having their conscience seared with a hot iron, forbidding to marry and commanding to abstain from meats, which God hath created to be received with thanksgiving of them which believe and known the truth".

What we see today in the world is the manifestation of darkness as stated in *1Tim.4:1 – 3*. But we should not be troubled because of it rather we should increase our capacity to learn from the scripture how we can manifest as light in this world. Our concern should be centred more on how we can change the course of the world by manifesting as light.

There is no volume of criticism, anger, hatred, debate that can change this act of darkness in this latter time. But let our energy concentrate on how we can manifest as light and effectively curtail or stop the activities of darkness in our world.

   (e) The next important thing to discuss from the same *Isaiah 60:1 – 4* is that the Lord shall arise upon Thee and His glory shall be seen upon Thee. If the Lord does not arise upon thee you cannot manifest as light. It is the Lord's light that will bring out the light in you.

From the story of blind Bartimaeus he did not arise until Jesus asked him to come. What he was doing and shouting was to attract Jesus attention and immediately he did that Jesus asked him to come.

We should Endeavour to attract Jesus into our life or the lives of others that is the only condition precedent that will enable us to shine as light.

Jesus coming unto the life of the woman of Samaria in John 4:28 – 30 made the light of God to shine upon her, with this light the woman went unto the city and the people gave heed to her saying about Jesus.

It is the light and glory of God that came upon the woman of Samaria that made the people who knew the terrible past of the woman to listen to her and follow her to see Jesus. Taking cognizance of the activities of darkness in the life of the woman of Samaria the people ought not to listen to her.

But the light and glory of God is so powerful to extinguish every act of darkness. It is so powerful to make a man or woman succeed where he or she had failed before or has the potential to fail.

With this light you that was a nonentity can become a known celebrity like the woman of Samaria. When Jesus comes in contact with any man or woman who truthfully receives him, that woman or man has the, potential to change the course of his destiny and the destiny of others just like the woman of Samaria did in her life and the lives of others.

Until the light of Jesus comes into you, His glory cannot be seen in you. The bible said in *Colossians 1:27* "To whom God would make known what is the riches of the glory of this mystery among the gentiles, **which is Christ in you, the hope of glory** Jesus in you or in your neighbor becomes the hope for His glory to be made manifest".

If you notice that God's glory is not seen in your life or you are not manifesting his glory then check your life to be sure that Jesus is in your life. We are not saying whether you attend a church or a fellowship. What brings glory manifestation in the life of a man is Jesus the light of the world in your life.

May be you have Jesus truly in your life but you do not give Jesus opportunity to light the world through you.

Just like the Ass Jesus sat upon during His triumphant entry into Jerusalem, you are like that Ass Jesus need to use to show his light and his glory to the dying world that have suffered so much activities of darkness.

Another example of Jesus light in the life of a man called Paul is seen in *Acts 9:3 – 6* "And as he journeyed, he came near Damascus and suddenly there shined around about him a light from heaven. And he fell to the earth, and heard a voice saying unto him Saul, Saul, why persecutest thou me? And he said, who art thou, Lord? And the Lord said, I am Jesus whom thou persecutest. It is hard for thee to kick against the pricks. And he trembling and astonished said, Lord, what will thou have me do? And the Lord said unto him, Arise and go into the city and it shall be told thee what thou must do".

You notice that Paul was an example of a man who was an embodiment of darkness. It is important to note here that even though Paul was walking in darkness; he never knew he was in darkness. Today we have men whom religious spirit had held them in bondage and they still think they are believers.

In *Act 9:1 – 2* "And Saul, yet breathing out threatening and slaughter against the disciples of the Lord went unto the High priest, and desired of him letters to Damascus to the synagogues, that if he found any of this way, whether they were men or women, he might bring them bound unto Jerusalem".

Saul now Paul was in full activities of darkness. While he was Saul he was working in darkness but at the time he encountered the light from above, the light introduced himself as Jesus and after that event Saul became Paul and became light of the world even till date.

Paul was learned as a lawyer, he was well informed in religious doctrine of Moses law but that was not enough for him to have the light of God and His glory. He could not manifest light and glory of God to the world. Rather he became an instrument in the hand of kingdom of darkness to kill those who believe in God through Jesus Christ.

The encounter of Paul with Jesus in Act 9 is an attestation that darkness cannot defeat light. Paul after encountering Jesus became a carrier of light and glory of God to the world.

What are you waiting for to encounter this wonderful God through Jesus Christ? It does not matter how dark a man or woman has become or the level of darkness manifestation in your life, Jesus coming into your life will make the difference.

He will change you or the person from a vessel of darkness to a vessel of light, He will change your life, bless you and make you a blessing to the world.

What are you waiting for? Jesus says in **Revelation 3:20** "Behold, I stand at the door, and knock: if any man hears my voice and opens the door, I will come in to him and will sup with him, and he with me".

Jesus is calling you now and if you are ready to accept him as your Lord and Saviour, stop now and with your whole heart repeat saying this prayer,

"Lord Jesus come into my life and be my savior and my Lord I Ask for your forgiveness for all my sins. I accept that I am a sinner and you came and died for my sins. Accept me today and help me to serve you all the days of my life. Thank you for accepting me in Jesus name I pray Amen".

(f) Another important issue to discuss in Isa. 60:1 – 4 is that the gentiles shall come to thy light and kings to the brightness of thy rising. God had declared that Gentiles (unbelievers) shall come to our light. We know that you don't beg ants to fly to a light bulb when it is on. But no matter how big a light bulb is and the light is not on, the ants will never fly to it.

For the Gentiles to come to our light we must be shining. It is not our size, qualification or wealth that will attract the gentiles. It goes further to mean that we may have rich testimonies with evidence to show but if our lifestyle does not conform to the image of God and God's light is not shining through us, the gentiles will abhor us and never get attracted to our light.

It goes further to show that we should not envy any gentile that does not have the light of God in him. Any gentile that is not a light in the market place should be attracted to our light.

We have a responsibility to disciple any gentile no matter his position in government, business or the society. That gentile is accepted by God's ordinance to come seeking for the light of God in us.

When Joseph became a prime minister in Egypt, the bible recorded that different nations came to Egypt to look for food and that is how the brothers of Joseph came to meet him in Egypt. The reason why different nations were coming to Egypt was not because of Pharaoh but because the light of Joseph that was shinning in Egypt through the wisdom God gave him. As an apostle in the market place you are expected to shine where the gentiles shall see it and come to your light.

When a bulb shines it does not announce that I am shinning. Whenever you shine as an apostle in the market place people around you including the gentiles shall notice it. And if they discover that you have what they need they will come to your light. Light does not hide and it does not carry microphone and be announcing that I am light. Light only shines for all to see that it is light. When light shines it bring joy to all including ants.

Any hater of light is only darkness and that is why the absence of light is darkness. Wherever light is not shinning then darkness is having It's way. If you as an apostle in the market place is not shinning within the area of your influence it means that you have by omission or commission permitted darkness to prevail or dominate. If the gentiles are not coming to your light you need to check your life if the light of God is shining through you.

Many believers who are not walking blameless before God have dimmed their light and this has affected the attraction of the gentiles to their light. An apostle in the market place without shining as light cannot attract any gentile to himself and thereby inhibiting the word of God from being fulfilled. Today we are enjoyed by the word of God to live our life so that we can manifest as light of the world so that the gentiles will come to our light.

The second limb of this passage talks about the Kings to come to the brightness of thy rising. It is not only the gentiles that are expected to come to our light but the kings and those in authority should come to our light.

But they will not come if we don't have light. And if they have not been coming it could mean that we are not shining or our light is not attractive enough to bring a fulfillment of the word of God in our life.

What we have seen these day are situation where the believers, General Overseers of churches and fellowships and apostles in the market place running to "the light" (which sometimes may be darkness) of those in authority looking for one favour or the other without a corresponding word of God to them.

We have seen a situation where some of the apostles in the market place appointed into one governmental office or the other and these apostles in the market place no longer attend fellowship or church services. Some comes with various reasons and excuses why they will not be in fellowship or church service. We have witnessed occasion where the apostles in the market place after their tenure in office have became worst than infidels.

The opportunity God gives us as apostles in the market place to be in government is that kings can come to the brightness of our light see ***Daniel 2:46 - 48*** "Then the king Nebuchadnezzar fell upon his face and worshipped Daniel and commanded that they should offer an oblation and sweet odours unto him. The king answered unto Daniel and said, of a truth it is that your God is a God of gods and a Lord of kings and a revealer of secrets seeing thou couldest reveal this secret. Then the king made Daniel a great man, and gave him many great gifts and made him ruler over the whole province of Babylon and chief of the governors over all the wise men of Babylon".

The king was attracted by the brightness of Daniel. What bring brightness is light, so the absence of light does not brighten any environment. So when the light of God is found in you, your brightness will radiate to the point that people including those in government will be attracted to your light.

Apostles in the market place are you in government parastatals or offices and people are not attracted to your brightness. Something is wrong. We need the brightness in the market place which will lighten the way of the kings and the gentiles. In ***Kings 10:1-2*** "And when the queen of Seba heard of the fame of Solomon concerning the name of the Lord, she came to prove him with hard questions. And she came to Jerusalem with a very great train with camels that bare spices and very much gold and precious stones and when she come to Solomon, she communed with him of all that was in her heart".

After the queen of Sheba came to Solomon she made the following remarks in ***1Kings 10:6-7*** "And she said to the king, it was a true report that I heard in mine own land of thy acts and of thy wisdom. Howbeit I believed not the words, until I came and mine eyes had seen it, and behold the half was not told me. Thy wisdom and prosperity exceedeth the fame which I heard".

It is not enough that you are dining with those in authority, if your light is not touching them, if your brightness is not attracting them, you are not manifesting as the light of the world.

Are you holding one position or the other, it does not matter how small the position is but kings and gentiles are not coming to you brightness, it means either you are not shinning or your light is dimmed that nobody is attracted to your brightness.

God's word cannot be broken, if God had said that kings shall come to the brightness of our light that is how it will be. As apostles in the market place we are the people, God was referring to in Isa. 60 that kings and gentiles shall come to our light.

We need to be what God has ordained that we should be otherwise we are not fulfilling our destiny. That you are a professional, a career man or woman, a business man or woman is only a platform God set for you to manifest as light as apostle in the market place.

The market place is your pulpit, is your evangelism ground; it is your mission work. Whatever name you want to give it does not matter but what matters is, are people in that field or in the market place getting attracted to your light, are kings and gentiles coming to your light in addition to your professional expertise.

Remember we shall account how we lived our life here on earth. How we used the opportunities and platform God created for us to bring men back to him.

Have we missed it because of our crave for personal aggrandizement. God is still waiting for us if we can repent and retrace our steps and follow the path God had created for us to be the light of the world.

When as apostle in the market place your advice or counsel lacks the word of God in it, there is a problem in *Isaiah 8:20* "To the law and to the testimony, if they speak not according to this word, it is because there is no light in them."

A man may profess to be a Christian with all the physical attributes and gift of speaking in tongues but once his action or statement lacks the word of God continually it means there is no light in him.

We can xray our thoughts, words or action is it in line with the word of God but if it is not we don't need to go further justifying ourselves or giving excuses. We must retrace our step and follow the path that will help us to manifest as the light of the world that is our calling, that is our ministry, anything outside this as apostles in the market place does not have a place in our life and career.

Fulfillment of our life purpose is only when we manifest as the light of the world, when gentiles and kings shall be attracted to our light and the brightness of our rising.

Some people today started as the light of the world but the attractions in the world had made them to deviate. The bible described them as in ***Luke 11:35*** "Take heed therefore that the light which is in thee be not darkness."

The children of Eli started as priest of the Lord in the book of 1 Samuel chapter 1 and when it got to 1 Samuel chapter 2:12, it described them as ''Now the sons of Eli were sons of Belial; they knew not the lord''.

This should not be our story, as light of the world, may we continue to shine brighter and brighter as described in the Bible that the way of the righteous shines brighter and brighter.

Jesus had left us an example to follow. To be the light of the world and fulfill it in our life in ***John 1:9*** "That was the true light which lighteth every man that cometh into the world."

So if we are the light of the world it is our responsibility to lighten every man in the world that we come across in our life. Jesus had played his own part and left us with the word that we should be his witness in all parts of the world.

What are we going to witness for Jesus. We shall witness as light of the world. The apostle in the market place should be a burning and a shining light as stated in ***John 5:35a*** "He was a burning and a shining light"

From the foregoing we can deduce that God wants us as apostles in the market pace to be indeed light to the gentiles in ***Acts 13:47*** "For so hath the Lord commanded us, saying, I have set thee to be a light of the gentiles that thou shouldest be for salvation unto the ends of the earth."

It is a command from God that all of us who are believers and engaged in one profession or the other or one business or the other should be a light to all the unbelievers we come in contact with in the field of our endeavours.

The kind of light God wants us as apostles (Believers) in the market place is the type that produces salvation for the unbelievers (Gentiles). We are expected to shine to the extent that unbelievers around us should receive salvation from God through us. If we fail to shine as light among the gentiles as commended by God, it means that we are failing in our duties God has given to us.

It is also a command means we don't have a choice in the matter. The proof that we love God is by obeying his commandment and part of God's commandment to us in this present dispensation is to be a light to the gentiles.

As we become light to the gentiles apart from helping them to receive salvation there are other expectation God wants to see fulfilled in our lives see ***Acts 26:18*** "To open eyes and to turn them from darkness to light, and from the power of satan unto God, that they may receive forgiveness of sins, and inheritance among them which are sanctified by faith that is in me".

God has persuaded us to be light to the world; He has gone further to command us to be light to the gentiles and turn them from darkness to light and from the power of satan unto God. Let us as apostles in the market place be on our duty post to fulfill the mandate God has given to all of us.

Can we join Paul to say in *2Timothy 4:7-8* "I have fought a good fight, I have finished my course, I have kept the faith, henceforth there is laid up for me a crown of righteousness, which the Lord, the righteous judge shall give me at that day, and not to me only but unto all them also that love his appearing".

Barrister Favour Victory

CHAPTER SEVEN

ATTRIBUTES OF BECOMING A LIGHT

For a light to shine, so many components are involved. It is the components that produce the light and it is the same components that keep the light shining.
Once there is damage to any of the components the light will not shine or it will not keep on shinning for example if there is electricity current in a house and there is no bulb to bring out the light, the house or office will still remain in darkness. May be the bulb is there but there is no electricity in the house or office there will be no light shinning in the place.

As it is in the physical so it is in the spiritual. God desires that we shall be the light of the world. He went further to command us to be light to the gentiles but there are spiritual components that will produce the light in us and there are spiritual components that will keep the light shinning.

In *Leviticus 24:2* "Command the children of Israel, that they bring unto thee pure oil olive beaten for the light to cause the lamps to burn continually". For the light to remain burning there must be oil, if there is no oil, the light has an expiry time or date.

The importance of oil to light cannot be over emphasized as we see in *Matthew 25:4* "Then shall the kingdom of heaven be likened unto ten virgins which took their lamps and went forth to meet the bridegroom. And five of them were wise and five were foolish. They that were foolish took their lamps and took no oil with them. But the wise took oil in their vessels with their lamps."

All the ten girls involved in this passage were all virgins but what distinguished the five from the other five virgins is the ability to carry extra oil while they are waiting for the coming of the bridegroom. The five virgins waited for bridegroom but what disqualified from entering in to dine with the bridegroom was there failure to carry an extra oil, when it matters for them to dine with the bridegroom they went looking for oil".

In *Matthew. 25:8* "And the foolish said unto the wise, give us of your oil, for our lamps are gone out". It is important to note that our lamp can go out and if that happens, our light will equally go out. To avoid our light from going out we must do what the five wise virgins did by carrying the oil and that was what guaranteed a place for them with the bridegroom when he arrived.

What is this oil the bible is referring to in *Matthew 25:1-4* "There is always a connection between the oil and the light as it was in the old testament see *Exodus 35:14, 28* "The candlestick also for the light and his furniture and his lamps, with the oil for the light"? And spice and oil for the light, and for the anointing oil, and for the sweet incense".

The oil is the liquid substance that helps physical light to shine. It is the substance that sustains the shinning of the light. In modern times it is referred as the electricity that supplies current to light without which there would be darkness.

If you must shine as light you also require oil. The oil referred is the anointing that comes by the manifestation of the Holy Spirit, without the Holy Spirit you cannot shine as light. Before Jesus started to manifest as the light of the world, He received the Holy Spirit by conception and He received the Holy Spirit to be empowered to shine as light of the world.

At conception Jesus had the Holy Spirit that is how every apostles in the market place received a measure of the Holy Spirit when He becomes born again, which is referred to as the spirit of Christ. But this is not enough if you must function effectively as an apostle in the market place.

Just as Jesus received the Holy Spirit by baptism for preparation of His ministry that is how all apostles in the market must receive the Holy spirit in order to actualize his divine purpose at the market place in **Matthew. 3:16-17** "And Jesus when he was baptized, went up straightway out of the water, and lo the heavens were opened unto him and he saw the spirit of God descending like a dove, and lighting upon him, and lo a voice from heaven, saying, this is my beloved son, in whom I am well pleased".

After Jesus was baptized by the Holy Spirit, you noticed that from hence Jesus activities were controlled by the leading of the Holy spirit this we can see in **Matthew. 4:1** "Then was Jesus led up of the spirit into the wilderness to be tempted of the devil". Jesus activities in the market place became regulated by the leading of the Holy Spirit.

Remember that majority act of Jesus was done in the market place. He became the first apostle in the market place. Jesus did not come from the priestly family of Levi but He came from the kingly family of Judah. His father was professional carpenter who was already in market place before Jesus was physically born. Jesus was raised by a carpenter See **Luke 4:26b** "And they said, is not this Joseph son?"

Jesus went about the cities and in the market place preaching the kingdom of God. **Luke 4:43** "And He said unto them, I must preach the kingdom of God to other cities also, for therefore am I sent".

Because Jesus operated in the power of the Holy Ghost the bible said He went about doing good. Where? I know in the market place in **Acts 10:38** "How God anointed Jesus of Nazareth with the Holy Ghost and with power, who went about doing good and healing all that were oppressed of the devil, for God was with him".

When Jesus finished his physical work here on earth before his departure to heaven He left an important instruction to his apostles, incidentally were professionals apostles in the market place and we that are hearing his word **Luke 24:49** "And behold, I send the promise of my father upon you. But tarry ye in the city of Jerusalem until ye be endued with power from on high."

Also in ***Acts 1:8*** "But ye shall receive power, after that the Holy Ghost is come upon you and ye shall be witnesses unto me both in Jerusalem and in all Judea and in Samaria and unto the uttermost part of the earth".

What Jesus is saying in essence is that as apostles in the market place we cannot be the light of world without the power and presence of the Holy Spirit. We cannot fulfill our function in the kingdom of God without the power and leading of the Holy Spirit.

If Jesus cannot do without the Holy Spirit, no apostle in the market place can do anything meaningful without the power and presence of the Holy Spirit.

So Jesus had left for us an example to follow if we must achieve success in the task God had given us.

Today what is required from us is not enough if we depend on the measure of the Holy Spirit we receive when we become born again. We must proceed to have the full measure of the Holy Spirit by the baptism of the Holy Spirit.

Apart from receiving the baptism of the Holy Spirit we must do to maintain an atmosphere the Holy Spirit will operate through us. That atmosphere that makes the Holy Spirit operate constantly in our lives is what we can liken to the oil to the light.

Note that Jesus has a secret that made him to succeed. That is the same secret God had revealed to us through the scripture which is emphasized in this book that secret lies in two scriptures which we shall look at and discuss on them.

First is in ***Act 10:38*** "how God anointed Jesus of Nazareth with the Holy Ghost and with power: who went about doing good, and healing all that were oppressed of the devil, **for God was with Him**".

The secret why Jesus succeeded in His life and ministry lies in that fact that "God was with Him". This is the four words that guarantee success to any man who have discovered it.

It is not just enough to be baptized with the Holy Spirit though very important and with the foundation of receiving the power and presence of God but this is not just enough there must be a perpetual presence of God to guarantee success.

Without the presence of God you cannot do good neither can you heal anybody. It is the presence of God in your life in the market place that will guarantee success for you in the area of your business and also in the area of your ministry.

Jesus is God and at the time He came to the earth He was God in John 1:1 "in the beginning was the word and the word was with God, and the word was God". Looking at Jesus as being God one would have expected him not to desire the presence of Almighty God. But Jesus knew that the key to success in all endeavors is the presence of God in one's life, one's business, marriage, finance, work, children, and health. In anything you are doing whether secular or spiritual that has God presence in it must succeed.

He attracted God's presence to himself in other to be an effective light to the world. In *Luke 2:22* "A light to lighten the Gentiles, and the glory of thy people Israel". *John 1:9* "That was the true light, which lighteth every man that cometh into the world".

But Jesus knew that every light has need for oil both for the shinning of the light and also for the sustenance of the light.

Jesus went for his own oil or what we may call the extra oil which said oil is found in the last paragraph of *Act 10:38* "... for God was with him". These four words became the oil Jesus needed to effectively do good and heal all those that have infirmities.

Jesus worked effectively and efficiently in the market place. He was able to be the light of the world. The people even testified to the fact that Jesus had this oil called "for God was with him". You see *John*

3:2 "The same came to Jesus by night and said him, Rabbi, we know that thou art a teacher come from God: For no man can do these miracles that thou doest, except God be with him".

It is not just enough to say that you have the oil called "for God was with him". People around must see this oil, if they don't see this oil they will not be attracted to your light and they will not come to the brightness of your rising.

This is not what you can manipulate, exaggerate or pretend to have it. If you have it you don't hide it, and you cannot hide it when you have this oil, you will know that you have it and people around you will know that you have it.

You don't struggle to shine as light when you have this oil. If you are still struggling to shine in the market place as an apostle it means you don't have it or you did not take extra oil like the foolish virgins.

This oil it is not a once experience, it is experience that will be part of your lifestyle until you are raptured into heaven.

Jesus knew the secret before he came here on earth that is why it is not compulsory that he must come from a priestly family.

What matters in your functionality in the market place is not the origin of your birth either from a priestly family or kingly family. What matters is that can you discover the secret of Jesus success and applies it to your ministry and life.

The second secret of Jesus success can also be found in two scripture **Psalm. 45:7** "Thou lovest righteousness and hatest wickedness: therefore God, thy God hath anointed thee with the oil of gladness above thy fellows". Also in **Hebrew. 1:9** "Thou hast loved righteousness, and hated iniquity; therefore God, even thy God, hath anointed thee with the oil of gladness above thy fellow".

This is another secret that made Jesus to succeed in His ministry and life that secret is called "righteousness". The Bible said Jesus loved righteousness because of his love for righteousness and his hatred for iniquity or wickedness God first of all anointed him with power and oil of gladness and therefore elevated him above his fellows.

See *Matthew. 4:10* "Then saith Jesus unto him, get thee hence, for it is written, thou shalt worship the lord thy God, and him only shalt thou serve".

Jesus was tempted like any other person not in the church but Jesus was tempted by the enemy in the market place. But the love He has for righteousness and hatred for iniquity granted him victory over the enemy and God elevated him.

The God we serve is holy so without holiness God's presence will not abide in you in *1Peter 1:15 – 16* "But as he which hath called you is holy, so be ye holy in all manner of conversation. Because it is written, be ye holy, for I am holy".

No one can accomplish much without the presence of God and if you need to accomplish much you must be prepared to remain holy for God to work in your life and work through you.

The two secret to success Jesus exhibited "The presence of God" and love for righteousness (Holiness) work together. None will be effective without the other.

It is the love of holiness or righteousness that attracts the presence of God see *Daniel 1:8* "But Daniel purposed in his heart that he would not defile himself with the portion of the king's meat, nor with the wine which he drank: therefore he requested of the prince of the eunuch that he might not defile himself. Now God had brought Daniel into favour and tender love with the prince of the eunuchs".

Perhaps the reason you are not receiving favour and tender love in the market place is because you have defiled yourself as an apostle in the market place or you are still defiling yourself.

Note that it is God not man that brings any man into favour and tender love with others. You may be hiding as an apostle in the market place, defiling yourself and believing that others in your office, neighborhood or the market place do not know you as a believer or an apostle in the market place. But know that God who rewards every man in his place of assignment knows who you are and if the expectation of God is not found in you as an apostle in the market place you cannot attract God's presence that will usher you into favour and tender love.

So Jesus came and left an example for us who are alive to follow. There were men in the past who followed this principle and became a champion at the market place.

David was one of those who treasured the presence of God; it was this presence of God that David had which he presented to Saul as His qualification to fight Goliath. *1Samuel 17:36 – 37* "Thy servant slew both the Lion and the Bear: and this uncircumcised philistine shall be as one of them, seeing he hath defied the armies of the Living God. David said moreover, the Lord that delivered me out of the paw of the Bear; he will deliver me out of the hand of this philistine. And Saul said unto David, go, and the Lord be with thee".

When David was confronted with the fact that he wants to fight Goliath what was his qualification to fight a man that has been fighting from his youth, the qualification David presented to Saul was nothing but "the presence of God".

You can be sure that if David wasn't sure of the presence of God he wouldn't have gone to the battle against Goliath with a sling and five stones. It does not matter what is challenging you now or what you are challenging, the presence of God is very powerful to ensure victory and success for you.

Today many apostles in the market place who started well has lost their tract and could nor maintain stability in their life and career because they have lost the presence of God.

The presence of God is that oil that keeps your light burning and shinning. if you go into the market place or you are there without God's presence constantly with you then success cannot be guaranteed and you are likened to the five foolish virgins that did not carry extra oil.

Another man who carried the presence of God into the market place and had success is Daniel see **Daniel 5:11** "There is a man in thy kingdom in whom is the spirit of the holy gods, and in the days of thy father light and understanding and wisdom, like the wisdom of the gods, was found in him".

Daniel was able to know the dream of the king and interpretation of the dream because he carries with him presence of God. **Daniel. 2:19 – 20** "Then was the secret revealed unto Daniel in a night vision. Then Daniel blessed the God of heaven. Daniel answered and said, blessed be the name of God forever and ever: for wisdom and might are his".

In the case of the three Hebrew children they not only carry the presence of God, they attracted the presence of God into the fire were their enemies have
taken them. **Daniel. 3:25** "He answered and said, lo, I see four men loose, walking in the midst of the fire, and they have no hurt; and the form of the fourth is like the son of God".

The presence of God is what will bring light to you and that is what will keep your light burning and shining. The moment the presence of God disappears from your life as an apostle in the market place no Gentile or king will be attracted to your light or the brightness of your rising.

The next secret of success lies in your love for righteousness and hatred for iniquity or wickedness. In the life of Joseph we saw how his love for righteousness and hatred for sin brought the presence of God that guaranteed favour and tender love for him from Pharaoh.

Genesis 39:11 – 12 "And it came to pass about this time, that Joseph went into the house to do his business and there was none of the men of the house there within. And she caught him by his garment, saying lie with me: and he left his garment in her hand, and fled and got him out".

Joseph was confronted with a demonic proposal of retaining his job in his master's house in a foreign land by defiling himself with another man's wife. Joseph chose to love righteousness and hate sin.

Joseph summed up his love for righteousness as in ***Genesis. 39:9*** "There is none greater in this house than I, neither hath he kept back anything from me but thee, because thou art his wife: how then can I do this great wickedness, and sin against God".

Today we are expected to follow the footstep of Jesus as Daniel, David, three Hebrew children and Joseph did. It is the expectation of God from us as apostles in the market place. We cannot qualify to work for God if we do not have the same attribute. The Bible said in ***Amos 3:3*** "can two work together unless they agree?"

Until you agree with God to work in holiness in order to attract God's presence in your life, you cannot achieve much as apostle in the market place. The bible described us as holy people, in ***1Peter 2:5*** "Ye also, as lively stones, are built up a spiritual house, an holy priesthood, to offer up spiritual sacrifices, acceptable to God by Jesus Christ".

1Peter. 2:9 "But ye are a chosen generation, a royal priesthood, an holy nation, a peculiar people; that ye should shew forth the praises of him who hath called you out of darkness into his marvelous light".

As long as Adam love righteousness and hated iniquity he attracted God's presence to himself and he remained a light to the world but when he defiled himself by sinning he lost the presence of God and thereafter could not maintain his own market place (The Garden of Eden) which God gave him to maintain.

Your effective functionality at the market place can only be guaranteed when you love righteousness and hate sin and thereby attracting God's presence to you.

It is God's presence that lightens you and men and women can be attracted to your light. What followed Adam and his family was curse when he failed to be a light to the world. The same animals that he named and tamed became his enemies.

The light Adam had in him when God created him could not be sustained because of the lack of oil in his life; the absence of God presence in Adam caused lack of oil that sustains the light. It will not be good as an apostle in the market place to go the way of Adam, started well but do not have the oil (The presence of God) which can sustain the light.

So it expedient upon us as people God had called to be holy and to live according to the ordinance of God in order to attract His presence.

Our lifestyle as apostles in the market place should be exemplary according to the dictates of the word of God, that is only the condition that can make us shine as light in the world.

We need to be the reference point of the world pertaining to righteous living. The people of Antioch saw the character of the disciples of Jesus and called them Christians.

In **Hebrew. 12:1** "Wherefore seeing we also are compassed about with so great a cloud of witness, let us lay aside every weight, and the sin which doth so easily beset us, and let us run with patience the race that is set before us".

As apostles in the market place the only way we can lay aside every weight and the sin which doth so easily beset us is by living according to the word of God in **Romans. 12:2** "And be not conformed to this world: but be ye transformed by the renewing of your mind, that ye may prove what is that good, and acceptable, and perfect, will of God".

Barrister Favour Victory

CHAPTER EIGHT

BATTLES BEFORE BECOMING A LIGHT

God at the beginning of His creation, created us to be light and have dominion over God creatures. *Genesis 1:27 – 28* "So God created man in his own image, in the image of God created he him; male and female created he them. And God blessed them, and God said unto them, be fruitful and multiply, and replenish the earth, and subdue it: and have dominion over the fish of the sea and over the foul of the air, and over every living thing that moveth upon the earth".

Man was created to be the light of the world from the beginning but the same issue of not living righteousness and hating sin denied man the presence of God and the light of man quenched.

The extinction of the light of man gave in for darkness to prevail. *Genesis. 3:23* "Therefore the Lord God sent him forth from the garden of Eden, to till the ground from whence he was taken".

The dominance of darkness over man came into existence, the enemy took it from man see *Luke 4:6* "And the devil said unto him all this power will I give thee, and the glory of them: for that is delivered unto me; and to whosoever I will give it".

In order to recover this position there are battles to fight. These battles were part of God's declaration to man in *Genesis 3:15* "And I will put enmity between thee and the woman, and between thy seed and her seed; it shall bruise thy head, and thou shalt bruise his heel".

This battle did not start with the children of men. It started after God creation of heaven and earth see **Genesis 1:2** "And the earth was without form, and void; and darkness was upon the face of the deep. And the spirit of God moved upon the face of the waters".

The emergence of darkness did not start today neither did it start with us; it started after God's creation of the earth.

Darkness gave the first warning shot. If darkness did not fear God to attack what God created, it will not fear our face or title or position to attack us who are the light of the earth.

Since creation there has been a battle over the dominance of the earth by darkness.

Note that it was the emergence of darkness that led God to create light. So the reason why God created us and made us the apostles in the market place is to contend with darkness and rule over the earth.

The first instruction God gave to man was to subdue it see Gen. 1:28 "And God blessed them and God said unto them, be fruitful and multiply, and replenish the earth, and subdue it; and have dominion over the fish of the sea, and over the foul of the air, and over every living thing that moveth upon the earth".

Take note that the word subdue and dominion are all battle language. God knew from the beginning that as darkness contended with His creation, darkness will contend with the children of light.

If we must emerge as the light of the world we must be ready to contend with darkness that is prevailing over the world and the people.

We must note that if God did not permit darkness it will not come into existence see **Isaiah 45:7** "I form the light and create darkness: I make peace and create evil: I the Lord do all these things".

Though God allow the existence of darkness but it was not his intention that darkness should prevail over light. Today we see that the children of God who are the light of the world had allowed darkness to exist in the world see *Isaiah 60:2* "For behold, the darkness shall cover the earth, and gross darkness the people: but the Lord shall arise upon thee and his glory shall be seen upon thee".

Though God knew that there shall be the emergence of darkness over the people as it is over the whole world today. But God also made provision for us to arise and shine over the people that are in darkness. God's glory is the empowerment that we shall receive to shine in the midst of the darkness.

When God saw darkness in his creation he did not retreat back or gloss over it. He took an action and it is this action that God took that gave the earth victory over the dominance of darkness.

We are equally expected to take action geared towards having dominance over darkness in our life and darkness over the people. What did God do when He saw darkness in *Genesis. 1:3* "And God said let there be light and there was light". And God gave light dominance over darkness see *John 1:5* "And the light shineth in darkness; and the darkness comprehended it not".

For any man who indeed wants to be a light of the world there is a battle waiting to be fought against the kingdom of darkness and its representatives in the world.

We take a quick look at David and see how he became the light of Israel that subdued the representative of darkness that wanted to have dominance over Israel.

In *1Samuel 17:4, 8-10* "And there went out a champion out of the camp of the Philistines named Goliath of Gath, whose height was six cubits and a span. And he stood and said unto the armies of Israel and said unto them, why are ye out **to set your battle** in array? Am not I a Philistine and ye servants to Saul? Choose you a man for you and let him come down to me. If he be able to fight with me, and to kill me, then will we be your servants; but if I prevail against him and kill him, then shall ye be our servants and serve us. And the

Philistine said I defy the armies of Israel this day, give me a man that we may fight together".

This was the language of Goliath to the children of Israel. His desire is to go into personal battle against any Israelites army and he has confidence he will win the battle. Darkness is always boastful and over confidence in her ability.

This was the scenario where darkness came to contend over the armies of Israel in order to have dominion over Israel.

Both Saul and his armies were so afraid to contend with the darkness that has risen over them. This line of battle was not common to Israelites style of battle. That is why the kingdom of darkness sometimes engages in a battle that is uncommon to us or mankind.

But it does not matter whether the battle is common or not or whether the enemy of our life is trying to intimidate us and have dominance over our life or the world, the thing that stand sure is the word of God that said in **Daniel 11:32b** .. "But the people that do know their God shall be strong and do exploits". The only people that will shine as light in this world today among the apostles in the market place shall be those that know their God and definitely will do exploit. With this motivation David decided to go into the battle with the representative of darkness. *1Samuel 17:26* "And David spake to the men that stood by him saying. What shall be done to the man that killeth this Philistine and taketh away the reproach from Israel? For who is this uncircumcised Philistine that he should defy the armies of the living God.".

When Saul challenged David and wanted to know his pedigree to fight a man whom he described that has been fighting from his youth, David presented his C V (resume)as his knowledge about God and what God did in his life and what God is capable of doing to this darkness through him. David answered in *1Samuel 17:32, 37* "And David said to Saul let no man's heart fail because of him, thy servant will go and fight with this Philistine. David said moreover the Lord that delivered me out of the paw of the lion, and out of the paw of the bear, he will deliver me out of the hand of this Philistine. And Saul said unto David, go and the Lord be with thee".

David because he know God and know what God can use him to do, he had victory over darkness and emerge as the light of the world for the nation of Israel.

1Samuel. 17:50 "So David prevailed over the Philistine with a sling and with a stone and slew him, but there was no sword in the hand of David".

Your emergency as a light of the world cannot be without a contention over the kingdom of darkness. The reason been what we were told in ***Isaiah 60:2*** "gross darkness have covered the people all over world."

You need to fight this gross darkness so that the people who are under this darkness can see your light and come to it.

The world today is faced between two opinions over walking in darkness or waling in the light as it was in days of Elijah in Israel ***1King 18:21*** "And Elijah came unto all the people, and said how long halt ye between two opinions? If the Lord be God follow him: but if Baal then follow him. And the people answered him not a word".

The people of Israelites in the time of Elijah has become confused of which way to go. Is it the way of the Lord or the way of Baal. This is as a result of those in authority embracing Baal instead of God and doing things with all impunities without any corresponding punishment.

The people have seen the emergence of darkness perpetrated by King Ahab and his family as it is among our presidents, prime ministers, governors and ministers.

The people were confused because only those who follow the way of Ball got political appointment and Juicy contracts. The people were confused because every strata of the society is ruled by the activities of the agent of darkness.

In the eyes of the people it appeared that God was on leave and darkness has taken over the affairs of Israel. The people were confused because the testimony of the present day is far different from the testimony of God which they heard from their fore fathers.

The people were wondering is it the same God that did wonders in the land of Egypt that His temple in Israel have been taken over by the prophets of Ball and He keeps quiet.

The people were confused because the prophets of God in the land had gone into hiding and afraid to speak up for fear of been killed. The apostles in the market place that ought to be the light of the world have become obsessed with their business and economic profit.

That is the same scenario that is playing out now in our own dispensation all over the world.

The way the people were confused in the time of Elijah that is also how many people in the world today are confused because they do not know whether to follow the way of God or the way of the kingdom of darkness.

Could it be that the prophets of God in our dispensation with the apostles in the market place have chosen the way of personal aggrandizement to agenda of God's kingdom and allowing the dominance of darkness over the people waiting for the emergency of the light of the world the bible said in **Romans. 8:19** "For the earnest expectation of the creature waiteth for the manifestation of the sons of God".

It is this waiting that made Elijah to manifest and decide to go into battle with the kingdom of darkness. In **1King 18:22-24** "Then said Elijah unto the people, I even I only remain a prophet of the Lord, but Baal's prophets are four hundred and fifty men, let them therefore give us two bullocks and let them chose one bullock for themselves and cut it in pieces and lay it on wood and put no fire under and I will dress the other bullock and lay it on wood and put no fire under. And call ye on the name of your gods and the God that answereth by fire, let him be God. And all the people answered and said it is well spoken".

The people responded when Elijah decided that he will go into battle with the representatives of the kingdom of darkness.

When Elijah did that because he knows his God and knew what his God is capable of doing through him, he won the victory over darkness and became the light of the world in Israel. in *1King 18:38-40* "Then the fire of the Lord fell and consumed the burnt sacrifice and the wood and the stones and the dust and licked up the water that was in the trench. And when all the people saw it, they fell on their faces and they said the Lord, he is the God the Lord, take the prophets of Baal, let not one of them escape and they took them and Elijah brought them down to the brook Kishon and slew then there".

The victory Elijah had over the prophets of Baal made the people to come to his light and worship God and it also rain of abundance to the people of Israel In *1Kings 18:45* "And it came to pass in the mean while that the heaven was black with clouds and wind and there was a great rain".

The issue of battle with the kingdom of darkness can be a natural issue it can be a family issue, it can also be a personal issue.

It is the same principle or strategy that is employed to fight this darkness "Those that know their God shall be strong and do exploit". This is what we saw in the lives of the three Hebrew children see *Daniel 3:14-15* "Nebuchadnezzar spake and said unto them, is it true, O Shadrach, Meshach and Abednego do not ye serve my gods, nor worship the golden image which I have set up? Now if ye be ready that at what time ye hear the sound of the cornet, flute, harp, sackbut psaltery, dulcimer and all kinds of music, ye fall down and worship the image which I have made well but if ye worship not, ye shall be cast the same hour into the midst of a burning fiery furnace, and who is that God that shall deliver you out of my hands?

The three Hebrew children was engaged in a personal battle with the kingdom of darkness and refused to bow to the dictates of darkness chose rather to die than compromise their faith and worship in God.

After this battle we knew what God did on their behalf and for them. It was after this battle over darkness and the victory they secured that made them the light of the world. See **Daniel 3:28** "Then Nebuchadnezzar spake, and said blessed be the God of Shadrach, Meshach, and Abednego, who hath sent his angel and delivered his servants that trusted in him, and have changed the king's word and yielded their bodies, that might not serve nor worship any god, except their own God".

The king came to the rising of the three Hebrew children and the Gentiles in that country came to their light.

Daniel was another man who fought over darkness in the lion's den and had victory when he became the light of the Babylonians, **Daniel 6:11** "Then these men assembled and found Daniel praying and making supplication before his God".

So in **Daniel, 6:16** "Then the king commanded, and they brought Daniel and cast him into the den of the lions. Now the king spake and said unto Daniel, thy God whom thou servest continually, he will deliver thee".

Daniel fought the kingdom of darkness in Babylon that wanted to weaken his faith through prayerlessness. The key to any victory is prayer that is why they said prayer is the master key. The root of Daniel's victory is his prayer life which his adversaries wanted to weaken or stop so that they can have victory over him.

But Daniel understood that his power and success lies in his prayer life and refused to compromise in the place of prayer even as an apostle in the market place.

Any apostle of the market place that plays with his prayer life is playing with his victory and success. It is not only when you are a pastor or minister that you will improve your prayer life.

As an apostle in the market place your prayer altar must be on fire otherwise your enemies will bring down your business or work and water down your testimonies.

Today the enemies of the apostle in the market place like Daniel are still fighting against our prayer life with so many excuses, busy schedule, tiredness from work and other irrelevant issues that brings down our prayer life.

The onus is on us to resist it because these are daily battles we engage in against the kingdom of darkness in order to secure victory in every aspect of our life and shine as light.

In the case of Daniel when he had victory he became the light of Babylon. **Daniel 6:23** "Then was the king exceeding glad for him, and commanded that they should take Daniel up out of the den. So Daniel was taken up out of the den, and no manner of hurt was found upon him, because he believed in his God".

The manifestation of Daniel as the light and representative of God can be seen in ***Daniel. 6:26*** "I make a decree, that in every dominion of my kingdom men tremble and fear be the God of Daniel: For he is the living God, and steadfast forever, and his kingdom that which shall not be destroyed and his dominion shall be even unto the end".

We like Daniel are expected to refuse compromise in our life, face the battle and become the light God had destined us to be.

Barrister Favour Victory

CHAPTER NINE

PREPARING LAY MEN TO BE APOSTLES AT THE MARKET PLACE

I want to repeat for the purpose of emphasize a quote I referred to in my book "Market place evangelism (outreach) key to billion souls" where Dr. Billy Graham said "I believe one of the next great moves of God is going to be through the believers in the work place".

In the same vain Dr. Peter Wagner said "A Job becomes a ministry when God leads you into an area where you take the voice of God, the anointing of God and the biblical principal into the area with you as you work and minister".

Engr. Steve Olumuyiwa had this to say about the laymen "The church still largely considers that global market place a secular environment. The Christian business person who finds himself or herself in the market place is still largely regarded as a layman who has no claim to being a minister of the gospel"

In view of the foregoing it is pertinent to all that laymen has a great role to play in the work of the kingdom of God before the second coming of our Lord Jesus Christ.

The real battle the lay men face is not in the church but in their working place or business area or their homes.

Most of this laymen have failed because there was not enough preparation for the laymen to function as apostles in the market place. We have seen men in the church who see prayers, studying the word and righteous living as belonging to the pastors and Reverends. They believe that since they do not preach on Sundays or weekly activities there are no need to develop themselves spiritually.

But we know that the kingdom of darkness operation is more at home and working place than the church.

Recently we have seen our Christians brothers trusted with exalted position in the government or multinational company that at the time they left that office they equally left their bible and their Christian virtues. It is so dangerous because at this time they have become big men (men with wealth) and nobody dares to follow them up especially when they have not forgotten the Christian clichés like "you are blessed" etc.

It has become apparent that our laymen must be prepared to be the apostles at the market place. This preparation cannot be over emphasized if we must achieve God's purpose in our generation.

When Jesus was here, he left us with an example, He actually went after laymen like Peter, James and John but he did not leave them as laymen, he made them his apostles both in the market place and in the synagogue (the church).

Jesus has left an example for us to follow. He had laid the principles of turning laymen into apostles which if we must succeed we must follow suit.

No one become useful in any profession or the job unless he is trained. if we want to accomplish great success among our laymen at the market place we must train or prepare them for the responsibility assigned to them.

Other religion dutifully prepares their laymen to function according to the dictates of their religion at their market place. I must commend the Full Gospel Business Men Fellowship International Nigeria who took training of laymen a serious matter and most of us have received great training through this fellowship.

How do we prepare the laymen to become the apostles for God in their own market place?

a) **BORN AGAIN:** No man builds a house without laying a foundation. Any house no matter how big or beautiful it is without a foundation will definitely collapse or where the foundation is not solid or on a sandy ground will surely collapse.

So it is imperative that before we prepare a lay man to become an apostle of God in the market place he must be born again.

It is the reception of Jesus as Lord and savior into the life of the layman that qualifies him or her to become the child of God see John 1:21 "But as many as received him, to them gave he power to become the sons of God, even to them that believe on his name".

In **John 3:3** "Jesus answered and said unto him, verily, I say unto thee, except a man be Born Again, he cannot see the kingdom of God."

Why must a layman be Born Again? **Romans.3:23** "For all have sinned and come short of the glory of God". *Psalm.51:5* "Behold, I was shapen in iniquity, and in sin did my mother conceive me".

This is the position of every human being born into this world. We were all born in iniquity because all have sinned and come short of the glory of God.

In **Romance. 6:32** "For the wages of sin is death; but the gift of God is eternal life through Jesus Christ our Lord". The only hope for all born in iniquity is the acceptance of Jesus Christ in our life. **John 3:16,18** "For God so loved the world that he gave his only begotten son that whosoever believeth in him shall not perish, but have everlasting life.

He that believeth on him is not condemned but he that believeth not is condemned already because he hath not believed in the name of the only begotten son of God".

It is important that every person born into this world must be born again to avoid condemnation and receive eternal life.

b) BAPTISM OF THE HOLY SPIRIT

It is not just enough to be born again. Born again is the first most important relationship with God but there are other things that will make your relationship with God stronger and more rewarding.

Romans. 8:1 "There is therefore now no condemnation to them which are in Christ Jesus, ho walk not after the flesh but after the spirit.
From the above scripture, we understand that apart from being born again, you need to walk after the spirit. The question now is: how do you walk after the spirit?. This brings us to another important event in the life of the layman desiring to be an apostle in the market place. He or she must have the baptism of the Holy Spirit that is the only way he or she can walk after the spirit. The importance of the baptism of the Holy Spirit for the layman cannot be over emphasized. Jesus needed the Holy Spirit and received Him in His life and He helped Him in His ministry that is why Jesus also recommended Him for us.

In *Luke 24:49* "And behold, I send the promise of my father upon you but tarry ye in the city of Jerusalem, until ye be induced with power from on high". Also in *Acts 1:8*, "But ye shall receive power, after that the Holy Ghost is come upon you and ye shall be witnesses unto me both in Jerusalem and in all Judea and in Samaria and unto the utmost part of the earth". Jesus re-emphasized the need for baptism of the Holy Spirit and what the baptism of the Holy Spirit will do in any life that receives the Holy Spirit.

Every apostle of the market place is a witness for the Lord in every city he or she finds himself or herself or in any organization or company where he or she works.

Jesus stated that every apostle in the market place that wants to be relevant in his calling will need the power to contend for the faith at the market place. The only way this power Jesus is talking about in Acts 1:8 Can only come to a person is when the Holy Spirit comes into the person's life through the baptism of the Holy Spirit.

In preparing a layman to be an apostle in the market place it is expedient that we encourage them to receive the Holy Spirit outside been born again.

I never knew about the personality of the Holy Spirit until I read Benny Hinn's book on the Holy Spirit, thereafter the desire to be baptized in the Holy Spirit came and I received him and my life has never remain the same and will never remain the same again.
Some of the laymen don't know there is need for a Holy Spirit. In *Acts 19:2,6* "And it came to pass that while Apollos was at Corinth, Paul having passed through the upper coasts came to Ephesus and finding certain disciples, He said unto them, have ye received the Holy Ghost since ye believed? And they said unto him, we have not so much as heard whether there by any Holy Ghost… And when Paul has laid his hands upon them, the Holy Ghost came on them and they spake with tongues and prophesied".

There are so many of the believers or laymen in the church that have not heard about the Holy Spirit and there are many that have heard about the Holy Spirit and have not seen the need to have him.

It is important to let the laymen know the need for the Holy Spirit more than the pastors or minister have need because the laymen are the people who are contending for the faith at the market place from Monday to Saturday of every week.

No one can have victory in business, marriage, work place except by the power of the Holy Spirit. There are so much contentions in the world today engineered by the kingdom of darkness that we need a greater power to subdue them and this power is found in the Holy Spirit.

Remember part of God's commandment in Gen. 1:28 is for man to subdue the earth. God is aware of the contentions men and women will be facing in the world and declared that man should subdue.

God did not just give us a command but as a good God He provided for us the power that can help us subdue the earth and that power is what Jesus told us in Acts 1:8 so it is left with us to receive the said power and be more than a conqueror.

DAILY WALK WITH THE HOLY SPIRIT

To help laymen to be victorious it is not just enough to know and receive the Holy Spirit as many of us have received him.

But some of us are not putting him to work. We are not giving him room to express himself or manifest his power, up till now some are still arguing about speaking in tongues and other issues.

The Holy Spirit has gifts and fruit which He wants to manifest through us. The only way this can be possible is if we learn to walk with him in our daily endeavours **Romans. 8:1** "There is therefore now no condemnation to them which are in Christ Jesus, who walk not after the flesh but after the Spirit".

We need as laymen to learn to walk after the Holy Spirit that is the only way we can achieve success through power of the Holy Spirit in all our endeavours.

There are so many benefits for any person who after receiving the Holy Spirit decide to walk daily with the Holy Spirit in terms of work, word, prayer and daily living.

c) PRAYER

In *Luke 11:1* "And it came to pass that as he was praying in a certain place when he ceased one of his disciples said unto him Lord teach us to pray as John also taught his disciples".

We saw that John the Baptist taught the laymen he raised to follow him how to pray. People noticed that the disciples of John the Baptist can pray. They must have seen a demonstration of the prayer exhibited by the disciples of John, Jesus disciples was compelled to ask Jesus to teach them how to pray.

Jesus did not rebuffed the disciples rather he responded by teaching his disciples and us how to pray as recorded in **Luke 11:2** "And he said unto them, why ye pray, say our father which art in heaven, hallowed be by name, thy kingdom come, thy will be done, as in heaven so on earth".

Today we know that what gave rise to our Lord's Prayer is a demand made by one of Jesus disciples.

If John the Baptist taught his disciples and Jesus taught his disciples how to pray it means that every disciples or believer that must follow Jesus or be relevant in the kingdom of God must be taught how to pray.

Laymen who must be prepared to be apostles at the market place must be taught how to pray.

In recent time we have seen believers who are not tutored in the acts of prayer and because they cannot pray effectively they are now running after signs and wonder. In **Mark 16:17** "And these signs shall follow them that believe in my name shall they cast out devils, they shall speak with new tongues"

As a result of the above many laymen have fallen into the hands of false prophets and cannot fulfill their mandate at the market place.

We must come to the point that where we evolve a pattern or concept to train and teach the laymen how to pray. After Jesus taught his disciples how to pray, he also carry them along when he goes to the quiet place or the mountain to pray. This is because the only way to know how to pray is by praying as the only way to know how to drive is by driving.

When the disciples of Jesus mastered the act of prayers, miracles followed it. ***Acts 3:1-2, 7, 8*** "Now Peter and John went up together into the temple at the hour of prayer being the ninth hour. A certain man came from his mother's womb was carried, whom they laid daily at the gate of the temple which is called beautiful to ask alms of them that entered into the temple, And he took him by the right hand and lifted him up and immediately his feet and ankle bones received strength and he leaping up, stood and walked and entered with them into the temple and leaping and praising God".

The effects of prayers of the disciples of Jesus are many as recorded in the New Testament one of them is seen in ***Acts 4:31*** "And when they had prayed the place was shaken where they were assembled together, and they were all filled with the Holy Ghost and they spake the word of God with boldness".

It is the effect of prayers that made the disciples of Jesus to give it a place of importance in their ministry see ***Act 6:3 – 4***, "Wherefore brethren, look ye out among you seven men of honest report, full of the Holy Ghost and wisdom, whom we may appoint over this business. But we will give ourselves continually to prayer and to the ministry of the word".

To have an effective laymen that will indeed be apostles of the market place we must prepare them in the aspect of prayer because there is a saying that a prayerless Christian is a powerless Christian.

It will be fatal to send powerless laymen to the market place. This may account for the reason we have been having causalities among the laymen at the market place.

We should not only be interested in their tithe, seed faith, building offering, first fruit but we should train them so that the above listed items can be sustained and their lifes and family lifes can also be sustained.

The word of God summarized it in **1Thessalonians. 4:17** "Pray without ceasing" and ***Luke 18:1*** "And he spake a parable unto them to this end, that men ought always to pray, and not to faint".

d) THE WORD OF GOD.

In *2Timothy 2:15* "Study to shew thyself approved unto God, a workman that needeth not to be ashamed, rightly dividing the word of truth". It is important that part of the training we give to laymen to become apostles at the market place is to study the word of God.

This is the same instruction God gave to Joshua when He was recruiting him as an apostle in the market place see *Joshua. 1:7 – 8* "Only be thou strong and very courageous, that thou mayest observe to do according to all the law, which Moses my servant commanded thee: turn not from it to the right hand or to the left, that thou mayest prosper whither soever thou goest. This book of the law shall not depart out of thy mouth; but thou shalt make thy way prosperous, and then thou shalt have good success".

Every laymen operating as an apostle at the market place must have faith to effectively operate and they only way the faith can come is through hearing the word of God: we need to teach the laymen the need to study the word of God in order to have faith. Because without faith it is impossible to please God.

The reason why many laymen in the market place are not pleasing God or their conduct is not pleasing God may be as a result of not having faith to trust and depend on God for their daily life.

Apart from faith, the word of God is the sword of the spirit; if a layman in the market place must succeed he needs the Holy Spirit to work effectively but the Holy Spirit cannot work efficiently without the sword which is the word of God.

We need to teach the laymen about studying the word of God in order to help the Holy Spirit in them work efficiently and effectively.

The importance of laymen studying the word of God can be seen in *Act 6:3 – 4* "Wherefore, brethren, look ye out seven men of honest report, full of the Holy Ghost and wisdom, whom we may appoint over this business. But we will give ourselves continually to prayer and to the ministry of the word".

Despite the fact that the apostles were with Jesus when He was on earth, but they realized the importance of placing priority in the study of the word of God as part of their own responsibility.

Every layman that must succeed at his own market place must follow the example of God Almighty and our Lord Jesus Christ.

In *Genesis 1:2* "And the earth was without form, and void; and darkness was upon the face of the deep. And the spirit of God moved upon the face of the water".

God was not looking at the situation the earth had fallen into but He used the word of God to address and change the situation as you can see in *Genesis 1:3* "And God said let there be light: and there was light".

Our Lord Jesus when He was confronted by the devil in the wilderness, He also employed the power in the word of God to defeat the devil *Matthew 4:3 – 4* "And when the tempter came to him, he said, if thou be the son of God, command that these stone be made bread. But he answered and said, it is written man shall not live by bread alone, but by every word that proceedeth out of the mouth of God.

Teaching the laymen the importance of studying the word of God is needful; it is not enough to see them in our church, fellowship or Bible Study.

Let there be a conscientious effort to teach and encourage the lay men to teach and engage in the study of the word of God constantly.

e) COURAGE AND INTEGRITY

In *Joshua 1:6 – 7* "Be strong and of a good courage: for unto this people shalt thou divide an inheritance the land which I sware unto their fathers to give them. Only be thou strong and very courageous, that thou mayest observe to do according to all the law, which Moses my servant commanded thee. Turn not from it to the right hand or to the left, that thou mayest prosper whithersoever thou goest".

We must teach our laymen to be brave and courageous. Market place is not a place of bread and butter there are issues that may be frightening that requires courage to deal with. God saw ahead of Joshua as he is seeing ahead of the laymen and encourages Joshua to be courageous.

Any man without courage cannot put his faith to work. There are so many places God told us fear not. *Isaiah 41:13* "For I the Lord thy God will hold thy right hand saying unto thee, fear not, I will help thee".

It is courage that gave David Victory over Goliath in *1Samuel 17:11* "When Saul and all Israel heard those words of Philistine, they were dismayed and greatly afraid. "Saul and his soldiers are all professional warriors that have faith in their ability to execute the war and that is the reason why they were at the battle against the Philistine but when they saw Goliath the courage required to put their faith to work was not there and they became afraid.

But there was a young layman who was not a professional soldier but has courage and when he saw Goliath the courage in him arose and put his faith to work. See *1Samuel 17:36* "Thy servant slew both the lion and the bear and this uncircumcised Philistine shall be as one of them, seeing he hath defied the armies of the living God".

Every believer needs courage to survive in the world we are in today. A lot of issues are challenging the faith of the believers and only the courageous can stand and contend for his faith.

The trend today has made us to make our laymen to be dependent of our leaders. Some of them cannot pray for themselves or their families and believe that God will hear their prayers.

They have been made to believe that only when they pray or call the God of G. O. or pastor then they will receive answer. As if the God of their G. O. or pastor is different from the God they serve.

It is important we teach the laymen in the market place about courage so that they can be victorious at the market place.

Apart from courage, we need to teach the laymen about integrity. The church today is lacking integrity which by extension has affected the laymen in the market place.

In recent time people prefer doing business with non believers than with believers as a result of some terrible experience they had with so called believers.

We need to restore integrity as part of character formation in the lives of our laymen who are the apostles at the market place.

Let's teach our laymen that their word should be their bond so that the heathens can believe we are indeed the followers of Christ.

f) DISCIPLESHIP

Matthew 28:19, 20 (ESV) "Go therefore and make disciples of all nations, baptizing them in the name of the father and of the son and of the Holy Spirit teach them to observe all that I have commanded you. And behold, I am with you always to the end of the age".

It is Jesus command that before we send our laymen out we should ensure that we have discipled them. Any believer that is not discipled cannot stand long in faith in the midst of adversary circumstance.

Jesus left an example for us to follow. Before Jesus died on the cross he went about recruiting laymen he made his disciples. He spent about 3½ years discipling them and that was the reason after Jesus resurrection, his disciples took over and turned the world upside down.

The issue of discipleship is a big topic that is not the intention of this book to dwell on it. The most important thing to note in this is that we must make an effort to disciple our laymen if we want them to be effective at the market place.

What made Joshua to be an effective apostle at the market place was because he was discipled by Moses. What made Elisha to be a prophet with double anointing was because Elijah discipled him.

We know what happened to Gehazi who refused to be properly discipled by Elijah. This has become the lot of many laymen in the market place because of lack of discipleship or improper discipleship.

The church or fellowship should found a way to re-introduce discipleship in the church or fellowship program otherwise the next generation that may take over from the present one may be a calamity – God forbid!

So to avoid the calamity let us do the needful by discipling our laymen and teach them to do and observe all the commandments of God as written in the bible.

Barrister Favour Victory

CHAPTER TEN

THREE THINGS APOSTLES IN THE MARKET PLACE BECOMES TO THE WORLD

(a) They are the modern day melchizedek
(b) They are the world changers
(c) They are custodians of God's wealth.

(a) THEY ARE THE MODERN DAY MELCHIZEDEK
To understand this well we need to look at the man in the bible called Melchizedek in *Genesis 14:18* "And Melchizedek king of Salem brought forth bread and wine and he was the priest of the most high God".

The bible described Melchizedek as king of Salem and the priest of the most high God.

The apostles in the market place today can be referred to as the modern day Melchizedek because he is a king and a priest of the most high God.

In **1Peter 2:9** "But ye are a chosen generation, a royal priesthood, an holy nation, a peculiar people, that ye should shew forth the praises of him who hath called you out of darkness into his marvelous light".

The bible in the book of revelation referred to believers as king and priest see ***Revelation 1:6*** "And hath made us kings and priests unto God and his father; to him be glory and dominion forever and ever Amen".

Also in ***Revelation 5:10*** "And hast made us unto our God kings and priests, we shall reign on the earth". The bible said in the mouth of two witnesses a matter is established.

In this we have three different chapters of the bible declaring to us that God had made us kings and priest unto our God.

It is obvious from the above passages apostles in the market place are the kings and priests God had ordained to fulfill his kingdom purpose. The functions of being a king and a priest are not what we may dwell here extensively.

It is important to realize who God has ordained us to be in the market place so that we can function in that capacity effectively.

A king we know rules over a kingdom or have dominion over a particular geographic hemisphere. If God has called us into a market place ministry that is part of the kingdom God has given us to reign as king. But most of us have relinquished this position to the unbelievers.

A king we know is either elected or nominated by the people or authority that has power to do that.

The bible said in Ps. 24:1 "The earth is the Lord's and the fullness thereof, the world and they that dwell therein. It shows that God owns the earth and has the power to appoint kings over the earth.

Our ordination to be kings in the earth and within our area of influence is an ordination from God which we must treasure so much and help to propagate the kingdom of God.

Since kings are not expected to be poor it shows that if God had ordained us to be kings here on earth, it is not part of his agenda for the apostles in the market place to be poor.

Until a king though anointed, begin to reign as king, he will still be denied his entitlement, he may still be poor. Yes we are God's ordained king in the earth most is us are not reigning as king within our area of calling or market place. We are not really in charge. We have not started manifesting God's purpose.

The man Melchizedek was the king of Salem as the bible recorded, he was not just ordained by God to be king over Salem, but he was actually in power ruling over the people of Salem that was why he was able to meet with Abraham and receive tithe from Abraham.

It is not a spiritual kingship; it is an actual kingship that was reigning within his area of domicile. What does God expect from the apostles in the market place is to reign by God's principles as enumerated in the bible.

In *Revelation 5:10* "It was clearly stated that we shall reign on the earth. So if we are not reigning in our market place, we are not yet the king that God has ordained us to be.

We must look inwards and know why we are not reigning in our area of influence. Sometimes lack of courage have hindered us from coming out to reign.

Today in the political scene, most believers have heard the voice of Goliath in the political scene and like Saul and his soldiers are hiding themselves out of fear of Goliath. It took a man called David who knows that he is an ordained king must reign over his enemy that rose and defeated the enemy called Goliath.

By way of digression, we have observed today that if when men like David had risen to defeat the Goliath of their time in order to reign, it is the same Saul who could not kill Goliath that is chasing the life of David to kill. The same is happening now to the apostles in the market place, those trying to bring them down now are people from the same faith with them.

The bible said we have been ordained as kings not king (it is in the plural form not singular form). It is not for one person alone. If someone has started reigning as a king on his own market place, let's take a clue from him and intensify effort to reign in our area of influence. It does not call for us to undo and bring him down out of jealously or envy. Time Saul could have spent to seek God and reconcile with God and govern his people effectively, he used it in chasing to kill David as if David was his enemy.

David knew he has been ordained as a king when he met Goliath at the market place, he did not run back to prepare, he confronted Goliath on the spot that also quicken his rise to the kingship position.

Apostles in the market place, you are a king. Live your life as a king ordained by God. You cannot ascend to your kingship the same manner the people of the world does. You must learn God's principles of becoming a king.

A study on David and Solomon will help us as apostles in the market place to know how to ascend to our kingship position and reign in a manner that will please God.

We are also ordained as priest of the Most High God. What sustains our kingship is our priesthood. It is a function that the people of the old like David and Solomon did not enjoy except Melchizedek.

But the coming of Jesus and tearing of the veil that covers the Holy of Holy has given us entrance and access to the presence of God. We can now operate as a king in the market place as well as operate as a priest.

This ordination is not new God had done such thing in the life of some prophet like Jeremiah in the book of ***Jeremiah. 1:5, 10*** "Before I formed thee in the belly I knew and before thou camest forth out of the womb I sanctified thee, and I ordained thee a prophet unto the nations. See I have this day set thee over the nations and over the kingdoms to root out and to pull down and to destroy, and to throw down, to build and to plant".

A responsibility is placed upon us at the market place. The only way we can accomplish this effectively is by functioning as king and priest at the market place. What will make others to listen to our testimony is when we begin to function as priest at the market place and as well reign as a king.

Our generation of believers are blessed by reason of what God had provided for them. The people that served God before the death and resurrection of Jesus they were kings or prophets/ priests. But in this dispensation of apostles in the market place God had given us the rare privilege of becoming kings and priests at the same time.

It goes to show that in the market place issues that requires a priest to do, we are ordained to do it and matters that required kingly intervention, we are ordained to do it as well.

(b) **THE WORLD CHANGERS**
The apostles in the market place are what we called world changers. They bring different positive changes in the world. They are agents of transformation.

They are involved in the course of changing things in the world. We will look at few examples in the bible and look at few examples in the present day.

Let us consider Abraham as in *Genesis. 22:9-10* "And they came to the place which God had told him of, and Abraham built an altar there, and laid the wood in order and bound Isaac his son, and laid him on the altar upon the wood. And Abraham stretched forth his hand, and took the knife to slay his son".

Abraham was not a Pastor or a minister he was a farmer and what can be likened today as a businessman. He did not possess any seminary training rather he was just an ordinary man doing his business when God called him to be his apostle in the business environment now called the market place. God in the course of his walk with Abraham blessed Abraham and gave him a son through his aged wife Sarah.

Later God made a demand on Abraham that will cause a change in the history of mankind thereby making Abraham to be a world changer.

In *Genesis 22:16-18* "And said by myself have I sworn, said the Lord, for because thou hast done this thing and hast not withheld thy son, thine only son that in blessing I will bless thee and in multiplying I will multiply thy seed as the stars of the heaven and as the sand which is upon the sea shore, and thy seed shall possess the gate of his enemies. **And in thy seed shall all the nations of the earth be blessed**, because thou hast obeyed my voice."

Abraham became a world changer simply by obeying the voice of God. He was requested to sacrifice his beloved son gotten in his old age and he simply obeyed without questioning.

Many of us are where we are today as a result of our disobedience to God's demand on our life. We can be among the world changer, if we can obey the voice of God calling us to the task of soul winning in all the nations of the world.

God told Abraham in *Genesis 22:18* "That through Abraham's seed (child) shall all the nations of the earth be blessed.

We see a fulfillment of the above scripture in *Luke 2:10-11* "And the angel said unto them, fear not for behold, I bring you **good tidings of great joy, which shalt be to all people**. For unto you is born this day in the city of David, **a Savour** which is Christ the Lord". Also in *Luke 2:32* "For mine eyes have seen thy salvation which thou has prepared before the face of all people; a light to lighten the gentiles and the glory of thy people Israel".

See also *Matthew 1:20-21* "But while he thought on these things behold the Angel of the Lord appeared unto him in a dream saying, Joseph thou son of David, fear not to take unto thee Mary thy wife for that which is conceived in her is of the Holy Ghost. And she shall bring forth a son, and thou shalt call his name JESUS. For **he shall save his people from their sins.**

Jesus came as the seed of Abraham through whom all the nations of the world shall be blessed. That's God promise to Abraham as a world changer manifested through the birth and resurrection of Jesus Christ.

Another person to be considered here from the bible who became a world changer is Noah. The prophetic world that was upon Noah at his birth showed that he was destined to be a world changer See *Genesis 5:29* "And he called his name Noah, saying this same shall comfort us concerning our work and toil of our hands because of the ground which the Lord hath cursed".

Noah did not just become a world changer only because it was prophesised by his father but he paid the price to be what his destiny was meant to be. He became a world changer by paying the price as we see in *Genesis 6:8-9* "But Noah found grace in the eyes of the Lord. These are the generations of Noah: **Noah was a just man and perfect in his generation and Noah walked with God**".

Noah was able to found grace in the eyes of God to become a world changer because he was a just man and perfect in his (perverse) generation and he also walked with God.

So if you want to be a world changer in your generation you must strive to found grace in the eyes of God by being a just man and perfect in this generation you live and must learn to walk with God.

It also means no matter how perverse your generation is you can still be a world changer if you are ready to follow the footsteps of Noah.

How did Noah became a world changer first in *Genesis 6:13-14, 22* "And God said unto Noah, the end of all flesh is come before me; for the earth is filled with violence through them, and behold, I will destroy them with the earth. Make thee an ark of gopher wood, rooms shalt thou make in the ark, and shalt pitch it within and without with pitch, thus did Noah, according to all that God commanded him, so did he".

Noah and his children became the generation God used to start a new race on the earth which had existed till date. God used Noah to preserve both the human race and the animal race.

The second event that made Noah to become a world changer is found in **Genesis 8:20-21** "And Noah builded an altar unto the Lord and took of every clean beast, and of every clean fowl and offered burnt offering on the altar and the Lord smelled a sweet savour, and the Lord said in his heart, I will not again curse the ground any more for man's sake, for the imagination of man's heart is evil form his youth, neither will I again smite any more everything living as I have done".

After God released Noah and his family from the Ark to use them to start a new earth, Noah being grateful to God offered God a thanksgiving offering which made God to reverse the curse he had place on the earth bringing a fulfillment of what Noah's father said at his birth. "And he called his name Noah, saying this same shall comfort us concerning our work and toils of our hands because of the ground which the Lord hath cursed".

From generation to generation Noah had registered his name among world changers as an apostle in the market place. We can be what Noah was irrespective of what the world today has become.

The bible said that Noah was just and perfect in his generations. This Noah's generation is the same generation God described as been perverse and full of violence that God decided to bring it to an end.

Noah generations may have been worse than this generation. Noah did not have many people calling on the name of God as we have today. Noah did not have the indwelling of the Holy Spirit as we have today. Noah did not have salvation that came through the death and resurrection of Christ Jesus as we have today. Noah did not have bibles printed in different translations and devotionals as we have today. Noah did not have the opportunity of attending a mega church or fellowship as we have today. Noah's library do not have the stock of Christian literatures as we have today. Noah did not have the benefit of watching Christian messages through television and cable television, ipad, iphone, tablet as we have today.

Noah in the midst of this disadvantage position compared to what we have today, remain resolute and make his face to be like a flint as the bible describes it and remain just and perfect in his generation.

In the midst of activities demanding the attention of Noah, he did not allow himself to be swallowed up with activities of life. He did not allow the building of the Ark to affect his walk with God. He chose in the midst of the rat race in his time to walk with God.

The result of that sacrificial decision Noah took was he found grace in the eyes of God and became a world changer. You can be one today, for God is not a respecter of person but will be willing to make you a world changer in your market place if you will single yourself out from this generation and pay the prince Noah paid. You can be a world changer for good.

The third person I will consider from the bible to be a world changer is a man called Joseph. In **Genesis 37:9-10** "And he dreamed yet another dream, and told it his brethren and said, behold, I have dreamed a dream more, and behold, the sun and the moon and the eleven stars made obeisance to me. And he told it to his father, and to his brethren and his father rebuked him, and said unto him, what is this dream that thou hast dreamed? Shall I and thy mother and thy brethren indeed come to bow down ourselves to thee to the earth?"

Joseph had a dream that informed him that he is meant to be a world changer. Though there were conspiracy by Joseph brothers to stop the fulfillment of that God's purpose as you can see in **Genesis 37:18-20** "And when they saw him afar off, even before he came near unto them, they conspired against him to slay him. And they said one to another behold, this dreamer cometh. Come now therefore, and let us slay him, and cast him into some pit and we will say some evil beast hath devoured him, and we shall see what will become of his dreams". The concern of the brother is to see what will become of his dreams of becoming a world changer.

Your dream of becoming a world changer is only if you agree with your conspirators but where you refuse to work according to their dictate surely help will come from above to help you as it came for Joseph.

Despite the conspiracy against Joseph by his brothers it was said in **Genesis 39:2-4** "And the Lord was with Joseph and he was a prosperous man, and he was in the house of his master an Egyptian. And his master saw that the Lord was with him, and that the Lord made all that he did to prosper in his hand."

And Joseph found grace in his sight and he served him and he made him overseer over his house and all that he had he put into his hand.

Joseph remain undaunted in the pursuant of his dream from God to be a world changer. Even the lustful disposition of Potiphar's wife could not stop him from reaching his goal. God made Joseph to became a world changer after he had paid the price to be one.

In **Gen. 41:41-43** "And Pharaoh said unto Joseph, see I have set thee over all the land of Egypt. And Pharaoh took off his ring from his hand and put it upon Joseph's hand and arrayed him in vestures of fine linen and put a gold chain about his neck, and he made him to ride in the second chariot which he had, and they cried before him, bow the knee and he made him ruler over all the land of Egypt".

Joseph becoming a leader in the land of Egypt became the platform he needed to be a world changer. He not only rules or affect the lives of people in Egypt he also became the instrument God used to preserve lives all over the earth as we can see in **Genesis 41:56-57** "And the famine was over all the face of the earth. And Joseph opened all the store houses and sold unto the Egyptians and the famine waxed sore in the land of Egypt. And **all countries came into Egypt** to Joseph for to buy corn, because that the famine was so sore in all lands". The entire world benefited from the wisdom God gave to Joseph to preserve corn during the season of plenty.

Joseph's brother and family benefited from it and brought the dream of Joseph to fulfillment as we can see in **Genesis 42:6,9** "And Joseph was the governor over the land, and he it was that sold to all the people of the land, and Joseph brethren came and bowed down themselves before him with their faces to the earth… And Joseph remembered the dreams which he dreamed of them and said unto them, ye are spies; to see the nakedness of the land ye are come".

Joseph was nothing but an apostle in the market place but because the Lord was with him and made him to prosper in all that he laid his hand to do he became a world changer by preserving the lives of not only the Egyptians but the people of all the whole earth.

Joseph re-echoed this in his statement to his brothers in **Genesis 50:19-20** "And Joseph said unto them, fear not, ye thought evil against me, but God meant it unto good, to bring to pass, as it is this day, **to save much people alive**".

Another personality that became a vessel in the hand of God to become a world changer was Mary the mother of Jesus.

In **Isaiah 7:14** "Therefore the Lord himself shall give you a sign, behold a virgin shall conceive, and bear a son and shall call his name Immanuel".

It was prophesized that a virgin will be an instrument in the hand of God to change the course of the world. But no mention of Mary was made in that prophecy. Mary an apostle in the market place positioned herself to found grace in the eyes of God to become the world changer that Isaiah the prophet prophesied.

In *Luke 1:26-28* "And in the six month the angel Gabriel was sent from God unto a city of Galilee, named Nazareth, to a virgin espoused to a man whose name was Joseph of the house of David and the virgin's name was Mary. And the angel came in unto her and said hail thou that art highly favoured the Lord is with thee, blessed art thou among women".

Mary found favour with God and God indeed made her to become a world changer in *Luke 1:30-31* "And the angel said unto her, fear not, Mary for thou has found favour with God. And behold, thou shalt conceive in thy womb and bring fort a son and shalt call his name Jesus".

Today the effect of what God used Mary to do have moved from one generation to another and from one country to another.

Apart from the biblical examples of world changers, there are other men and women whose names are not written in the bible but have made a contribution that brought positive change to the world.

With permission I will refer to articles I got from the internet about Christians apostles in the market place that either invented things and did some things that affected the entire world.

The list below are famous scientists (market place apostles) who believed in God, copied with permission from godandscience.org.

    (1)   Nicholas Corpernicus (1473 -1543) Copernicus was the polish astronomer who put forward the first mathematically based system of planets going around the sun. Copernicus referred sometimes to God in his works and did not see his system as in conflict with the bible.

    (2)   Sir Francis Bacon (1561 – 1627) Bacon was a philosopher who is known for establishing the scientific method of inquiring based on experimentation and inductive reasoning.
Bacon established his goals as being the discovery of truth, service to his country and service to the church.

    (3)   Johannes Kepler (1571 – 1630) Kepler was a brilliant mathematician and astronomer. He did early work on light and established the laws of planetary motion about the sun.

    (4)   Galileo (1564 – 1642) His controversial work on the solar system was published in 1633. Galileo did his most useful theoretical work which was on dynamics. Galileo expressly said that the bible cannot err, and saw his system as an alternate interpretation of the biblical texts.

    (5)   Rene Descartes (1596 – 1650) Descartes was a French mathematician scientist and philosopher who has been called the father of modern philosophy. Rene Descartes and Francis Bacon (1561 – 1626) one

generally regarded as the key figures in the development of scientific methodology.

Both had systems in which God was important and both seems more devout than the average for their era.

(6) Blaise Pascal (1623 – 1662) Pascal was a French mathematician, physist inventor, writer and theologian. In mathematics, he published a treatise on the subject of projective geometry and established the foundation for probability theory. Pascal invented a mechanical calculator and established the principles of vacuums and the pressure of air. Pascal's last worlds were "may God never abandon me".

(7) Isaac Newton (1642 – 1727) in optics, mechanics and mathematics, Newton was a figure of undisputed genius and innovation. In all his science (including) chemistry he saw mathematics and numbers as central.

What is less well known is that he was devoutly religious and saw numbers as involved in understanding.

(8) Robert Boyle (1791 -1867) one of the founders and key early members of the Royal society Boyle gave his name to Boyle's law for gases and also wrote an important work on chemistry. Encyclopedia Britannica says of him. By his will be endowed a series of Boyle lectures, or sermons which still continue for proving the Christian religion against notorious infidels.

(9) Michael Faraday (1791 – 1867) Michael Faraday (1791 – 1867) Michael Faraday was one of the greatest scientists of the 19th century. His work on electricity and magnetism not only revolutionized physics, but

led to much of our lifestyles today which depends on them (including computers, telephone lines and websites) Faraday was a devout Christian.

(10) William Thomson Kelvin (1824 – 1907) Kelvin was foremost among the small group of British scientist who helped to lay the foundations of modern physics. He was a very committed Christian.

(11) Max Planck (1858 – 1947) Planck made many contributions to Physics but is best known for quantum theory which revolutionized our understanding of the atomic and subatomic worlds. Planck expressed the view that God is everywhere present. Planck was a church warden from 1920 until his death, and believed in an Almighty, all knowing beneficent God.

(12) Albert Einstein (1879 - 1955) Einstein is probably the best known and most highly revered scientist of the twentieth century, and is associated with major revolutions in our thinking about time, gravity and the conversion of matter to energy. Einstein expressed a belief in God.

(13) James clerk Maxwell (1831 – 1879) while still a young student of Cambridge he underwent an evangelical conversion that he described as having given him a new perception of the love of God. He is known for his contributions in establishing electromagnetic theory (Maxwell's equations) and work on the chemical kinetic theory of gases.

Apart from the ones listed above there are others that lived within the 19th and 20th century.

Currently we have men like Dr. Ben Carson (born 1951) American neuro surgeon. The first to successfully separate cojoined twins joined at the head. Dr. Ben Carson ventured into American politics in 2016 and contested in the primary election of the Republican party presidential race. Though he stepped down but he had carried his apostolic mandate to the political (market place) sphere of the American society.

There are other men and women who had used their God given gift to become world changers that this book cannot contain them though the theme of this book do not centre on them.

But the great lesson we need to learn from these men and women dead or alive is that; in that our given field or place of our professional calling we can be world changers when we found grace in the eyes of the Lord.

Remember creation is waiting for us to change things and become world changer see **Romans 8:19-21** "For earnest expectation of the creature waiteth for the manifestation of the sons of God …. Because the creature itself also shall be delivered from the bondage of corruption into the glorious liberty of the children of God.

God is waiting for you to be next world changer if you can be found faithful in the place of your calling as an apostle of the market place. God bless your endeavour. Amen.

(c) **THEY ARE CUSTODIANS OF GOD'S WEALTH**
Another remarkable thing about the apostles of the market place, they are the privileged few that God had made the custodian of his wealth.

It is not in doubt that God is rich not only in heaven but on the earth in **Psalm 24:1** "the earth is the Lord's and fullness thereof, the word, and that dwell therein."

If the earth and the fullness thereof belong to the Lord, there is no gain saying that all the wealth in the earth belongs to the Lord.

But I believe that in every generation God select among those that love him dearly and make them custodian of his earthly wealth.

We will consider few people from the bible as we are all living witnesses of some people in our society today that are custodian of God's wealth.

The first person we will consider is Abraham whom the Lord called and promised to make him a custodian of his wealth see ***Genesis 12:1-2*** "Now the Lord had said unto Abram, get thee out of thy country, and from thy kindred, and from thy father's house, unto a land that I will show thee. And I will make of thee a great nation; and I will bless thee, and make thy name great; and thou shalt be a blessing".

The bible recorded that God's promise to Abraham came to pass ***Genesis 24:1*** "And Abraham was old and well stricken in age, and the Lord had blessed Abraham in all things".

The evidence of Abraham's wealth can be seen in the following scriptures ***Genesis 24:10*** "and the servant took ten camels of the camels of his master and departed; for all the goods of his master were in his hand; and he arose and went to Mesopotamia, unto the city of Nahor".

Here the bible did not tell us how many camels Abraham had, that his servant took ten camels out of the camels Abraham had, speaks of great wealth. Even today any man that has ten camels or ten cars should be considered to be very rich.

In ***Genesis 24:22*** "And it came to pass as the camels had done drinking that the man took a golden earring of half a shekel weight, and two bracelets for her hands of ten shekels weight of gold." This is some gold that Abraham's servant took and gave Rebekah even before she accepted the offer to marry Isaac. The gold is part of the abundance of gold Abraham had.

Abraham's servant also testified about Abraham's wealth in ***Genesis 24:35*** "and the Lord hath blessed my master greatly, and he is become great, and he hath given him flocks, and herd and silver and gold and men servants and maidservants and camels and asses".

The manifestation of Abraham's wealth was displayed by the servant in *Genesis 24:35* "And the servant brought forth jewels of silver, jewels of gold and rainment, and gave them to Rebekah. He gave also to her brother and to her mother precious things".

The promise of God to Abraham in *Genesis 12:1* that he will make him a custodian of his wealth was fulfilled in the life of Abraham. God is faithful.

The next person we will consider is Isaac the son of Abraham though he inherited great fortune form his father Abraham it did not stop God from blessing him and making him a custodian of his wealth.

In *Genesis 25:5* "And Abraham gave all that he had unto Isaac." This scripture goes to encourage us that if we walk in the Lord and God blesses us, and if our children also follow our footstep, God will ensure that what he gave us, we can pass it unto our children.

But God is not bound to remain at inherited blessing. Apart from the inherited blessing God Can still give us fresh blessing different from what we inherited or increase on the inherited blessing. God started with Isaac with a promise in *Genesis 26:1-4* "And there was a famine in the land, beside the first famine that was in the days of Abraham. And Isaac went unto Abimelech king of the Philistine unto Gerar. And the Lord appeared unto him, and said, go not down into Egypt, dwell in the land which I shall tell thee of, Sojourn in this land, I will be with thee of; and will bless thee, for unto thee, and unto thy seed, I will give all these countries, and I will perform the oath which I swear unto Abraham thy father, and I will make thy seed to multiply as the stars of heaven, and will give unto thy seed all these countries, and in thy seed shall all the nations of the earth be blessed".

The promise of God to Isaac is nothing but announcing to him that he will be a custodian of God's wealth not unto himself alone but the entire race. In *Genesis 26:12-14* "Then Isaac sowed in that land, and received in the same year and hundred fold, and the Lord blessed him. And the man waxed great and went forward and grew until he became very great. For he had possession of flocks and possession of herds and great store of servants **and the Philistines envied him".**

The wealth of Isaac was enormous that the Philistines envied him. What is it that God had promised you, believe him and pay your price as apostle of the market place, you will definitely become a custodian of God's wealth to the point that people will envy you.

To discuss custodian of God's wealth without including the richest man on earth will not be complete and that man was not an unbeliever but another apostles of the market place his name is King Solomon.

1Kings 2:12 "Then sat Solomon upon the throne of David his father, and his kingdom was established greatly". Solomon by his act at the market place (political kingdom) God visited Solomon in *1Kings 3:5* "In Gibeon the Lord appeared to Solomon in a dream by night and God said, ask what I shall give thee". When Solomon eventually ask God for wisdom God answered him *1King 3:11 -13* " And God said unto him, because thou hast asked this thing, and hast not asked for thyself, long life, neither hast asked riches for thyself, nor hast asked the life of thine enemies, but has asked for thyself understanding to discern judgment, behold I have done according to thy words lo: to I have given thee a wise and an understanding heart, so that there was none like thee before thee, and I after thee shall any arise like unto thee. And I have also given thee that which thou has not asked, both riches and honour, so that there shall not be any among the kings like unto thee all thy days"

The fulfillment of the above promise and greater things the Lord did for Solomon to make him become custodian of God's wealth is recorded in 1 *King 4:22-34* "I will encourage you to read the scripture quoted above to see that when God gives you a promise, he keeps to it. God is waiting for you to position yourself to be his custodian of his wealth. God is faithful.

There are so many people in the bible time and space may not permit us to discuss about them as custodians of God's wealth but the last person to consider in this series is job.

In *Job 1:3* "His substance also was seven thousand sheep, and three thousand camels, and five hundred yoke of oxen, and five hundred she asses, and a very great household, so that this man was the **greatest of all the men of the east**". Job became custodian of God's wealth and God made him the greatest among all the men in the east.

It is important to note that in the time of Job, it was not an unbeliever or occultic man that was the greatest as it is erroneously believedin this present generation, it was Job that was the greatest. Job was also an apostle in the market place like any of us but what qualified Job to be a custodian of God's wealth in his own generation and time was recorded in Job 1:1 "there was a man in the land of Uz, whose name was Job, and that man was perfect and upright and one that feared God, and eschewed evil".

The wealth God place in the hand of Job was quite enormous that qualified him to be the greatest in the east. But God was not satisfied with that position and decided to increase his wealth.

God allowed Job to pass through another level of training which by the end of the training God double blessed Job and made him a reference point from his generation up till today.

In **Job 1:20-22** "Then Job arose and rent his mantle and shaved his head and **fell down upon the ground, and worshipped,** and said naked came I out of my mother's womb and naked shall I return father. The Lord gave, and the Lord hath taken away; blessed be the name of the Lord. In all this *job sinned not, nor charged God foolishly*".

The result of Job trial brought abundance to him and he remained the custodian of God's wealth. *Job 42:10* "And the Lord turned the captivity of Job when he prayed for his friends also the Lord have Job twice as much as he had before".

Job was a faithful apostle in the market place that was why God made him a custodian of God's wealth. Read *Job 29:1-25*. But we can see a glimpse of Job's activity in the market place in *Job 29:12 – 13* "Because I delivered the poor that cried and the fatherless and him that had none to help him. The blessing of him that was ready to perish came upon me; and caused the widow's heart to sing for joy"

Can we emulate Job as being a perfect man and who that fears the Lord and can we effectively mobilize our resources to help the poor, the needy, orphans and widows so that we can be a dependable apostle in the market place?

God is waiting for you to prove yourself that he can trust you with his wealth. How do you sow into the kingdom of God? How do you help those in need? If God cannot trust you with his wealth, he cannot make you a custodian of his wealth.

Now that you have read this book because God is no respecter of person but whoever that proves himself faithful the opportunity to became custodian of God's wealth is still open to you. GRAB IT.

Despite all these recorded in the bible. In our society today we can look around and see God's children who the Lord had made custodian of his wealth. Time and space will fail us to mention many of them in our society today.

But as God found you faithful to become custodian of God's wealth use it for the purpose it was meant for.

Remember that it is God that gave you power to make wealth. Let God's purpose and his kingdom be part of your agenda as you become custodian of God's wealth. God bless you.

CHAPTER ELEVEN

REWARD WHEN YOU BECOME A LIGHT

When God called Abraham to become the light of the world he told him that there is a reward for him. *Genesis 12:2* "And I will make of thee a great nation, and I will bless thee and make thy name great, and thou shalt be a blessing".

Also in *Genesis 15:1* "After these things the word of the Lord came unto Abram in a vision, saying, fear not Abram I am thy shield and thy exceeding great reward".

The apostle in the market place that became faithful in his calling stand to receive reward from God. But before this reward comes you must show forth that you are the light of the world.

In *Psalm 112:4,7,9* "Unto the upright there ariseth light in the darkness he is gracious and full of compassion and righteous. He shall not be afraid of evil tidings; his heart is fixed trusting in the Lord. He hath dispersed, he hath given to the poor, his righteous endureth forever, and his horn shall be exalted with honours".

From the above scripture we can deduce the following rewards for an apostle that has arisen as light in the darkness.

(a) There is character formation that makes him gracious, compassionate and righteous. These are virtues that will attract God's blessing to him. With these virtues we will find favour with God and with man above all, his eternal life is guaranteed because he is righteous.

(b) The apostle in the market place is not afraid of evil tidings, evil or bad report. He does not expect evil report or bad report as affecting his life, marriage, children, business and ministry.

His heart is fixed that even when unpleasant incident happens he knows that it will turn out good for him because of **Romans 8:28** "All things works together for good to them that love God".

(c) The apostle's horn shall be exalted with honour. We remember the story of Daniel in the land of Babylon. Despite all that the enemies of Daniel tried to do to him, God caused Daniel's horn to be exalted with honour **Daniel. 6:28** "So this Daniel prospered in the reign of Danuis and in the reign of Cyrus the Persian".

God has different ways he blessed his apostles in the market place who became light to the world. You will see that the way God blessed Daniel was different from the way he blessed Mordecai, Esther and Joseph. But the most important thing is that in your field of endeavour God had promised to exalt your horn with honour.

In considering the rewards that apostles of the market place received we will look at the scripture in **Isaiah. 58:8-12, 14** "Then shall thy light break forth as the morning and thine health shall spring forth speedily: and thy righteous shall go before thee, the glory of the Lord shall be thy reward.

Then shall thou call, and the Lord shall answer, thou shalt cry, and he shall say here I am. If thou take away from the midst of thee the yoke, the putting forth of the finger, and speaking vanity.

And if thou draw out thy soul to the hungry, and satisfy the afflicted soul, then shall thy light rise in obscurity and thy darkness be as the noonday. And the Lord shall guide thee continually and satisfy thy soul in drought and make fat thy bones and thou shalt be like a watered garden and like a spring of water, whose waters fail not.

And they that shall be of thee shall build the old waste places, thou shalt raise up the foundations of many generations, and thou shalt be called the repairer of the breach, the restorer of paths to dwell in.

Then shalt thou delight thyself in the Lord, and I will cause thee to ride upon the high places of the earth and feed thee with the heritage of Jacob thy father, for the mouth of Lord hath spoken it".

The reward of the apostles in the market place can be seen in many bible verses which include *Isaiah 60:4-22* and **Daniel 2:46-48.** Because of time and space we many re-emphasis the rewards outlined in *Isaiah 58:8-12, 14*.

From the scripture above we noticed that once your light break forth in your area of market place, then your health shall spring forth. You are expected to enjoy divine health as apostles of the market place your light break forth. That is the reason you see some of us from year to year we are not admitted in any hospital.

Once sickness comes, prayer we pray to God will bring healing. Sometimes you will stay months and years without experiencing any sickness which is according to *3John 2* "Beloved, I wish above all things that thou mayest prosper and be in health, even as thy soul prospereth.

Another reward you shall receive when you become the light of the world as apostles in the market place is the glory of God becomes your reward. This is the same glory of God Moses desires to have earnestly. Stephen was opporturned to see the glory of God in his short stay here on earth as recorded in *Acts 7:55* "But he being full of the Holy Ghost looked up steadfastly into heaven and saw the glory of God, and Jesus standing on the right hand of God".

What the glory of God does in the life of a man is so many that we cannot enumerate all here but the glory of God most often attracts divine favour that will make every man that comes across you to favour you.

Another reward you will get is when you call upon God for challenges or issues facing you, God will answer you **Psalm 50:15** "And call upon me in the day of trouble, I will deliver thee, and thou shall glorify me".

Also in **Jeremiah 33:3** "Call unto me and I will answer thee, and show thee great and mighty things which thou knowest not". God is prepared to hear us anywhere, anytime for anything when we become the light as apostles in the market place.

God also promised to guide us continually and satisfy our soul. In **2Peter 1:3** "According as his divine power hath given unto us all things that pertain unto life and godliness through the knowledge of him that hath called us to glory and virtue".

All that we need here on earth has been provided by the Lord. It is left for us to position ourselves in order to access these blessings pertaining to life which God provided for us.

Your blessing as apostles in the market place does not depend upon the economy of the nation you belong to, God has a way of providing for you even in the midst of draught or famine in **Psalm 3:1** "And he shall be like a tree planted by the rivers of water that bringeth forth his fruit in his season, his leaf also shall not wither and whatsoever he doeth shall prosper".

We will consider the reward of some apostle in the market place who became a light to the world.

We will briefly consider Joseph a man who was sold into Egypt as slave. But did not allow the spirit of captivity to blind him from manifesting as light in his market place. The end result of Joseph attitude was becoming a prime minister in Egypt, this was the reward God gave him in a foreign land **Genesis 41:39 -40** "And Pharaoh said unto Joseph, forasmuch as God hath shewed thee all this, there is none so discreet and wise as thou art. Thou shalt be over my house and according unto thy word shalt all my people be ruled only in the throne will I be greater than thou".

Another man who received rewards as a result of becoming a light to the world in his market place was Daniel. A captive brought into Babylon but that did not stop his light from shinning in Babylon and God honoured him. In ***Daniel 2:46 – 48*** "Then the king Nebuchadnezzar fell upon his face and worshipped Daniel and commanded that they should offer an oblation and sweet odours unto him. The king answered unto Daniel and said of a truth it is that your God is a God of gods, and a Lord of kings, and a revealer of secrets seeing thou couldest reveal this secret then the king made Daniel a great man, and gave him many great gifts, and made him ruler over the whole province of Babylon and chief of the governors over all the wise men of Babylon"

As apostles in the market place I encourage you to be light wherever you find yourselves. You are indeed working for a God that reward is associated with service unto him ***Colossians 3:24*** "Knowing that of the Lord ye shall receive the reward of the inheritance for ye serve the Lord Christ".

Revelation 22:12 "And behold, I come quickly, and my reward is with me, to give every man according as his work shall be".

Barrister Favour Victory

CHAPTER TWELVE

PRACTICAL EXAMPLE OF BEING A LIGHT OF THE WORLD

Genesis 1:2 -3 "And the earth was without form and void, and darkness was upon the face of the deep. And the spirit of God moved upon the face of the waters. And God said let there be light and there was light".

God left us with a practical way of bringing light to the dying world. He saw there was darkness over the whole earth, instead of complaining he introduced light into the earth. Henceforth declared that we are the light of world.

When Jesus came to the earth he continued with that message we are the light of the world.

How do we manifest the light in the world? What are the practical examples left for us to follow?

We may be considering the examples of people like Joseph, Moses, Paul, Esther, David and the Hebrew children.

JOSEPH

Even though Joseph was a slave in the house of Potiphar but he radiated the light of God. It became obvious to everybody that Joseph presence in Potiphar's house also attracted God's presence which brought prosperity.

Genesis 39:2-3 "And the Lord was with Joseph and he was a prosperous man, and he was in the house of his master the Egyptian. And his master was that the Lord was with him, and that the Lord made all that he did to prosper in his hand".

Joseph further manifested the light of God in his life in the prison see ***Genesis 39:21-23*** "But the Lord was with Joseph and shewed him mercy and give him favour in the sight of the keeper of the prison. And the keeper of the prison committed to Joseph's hand all the prisoners that were in the prison, and whatsoever they did there, he was the doer of it. The keeper of the prison looked not to anything that was under his hand, because the Lord was with him, and that which he did, the Lord made it to prosper".

From the above scripture we discovered that Joseph continues to manifest as light irrespective of his circumstances or where he found himself.

Even where things does not seem to favour us, we are encouraged to manifest the light of God in us. Joseph was not depressed by circumstances but he overcame his depressed situation by continues attracting God's presence in his life which gave rise to Joseph manifesting as light to his world.

Your world is now where you find yourself. You are not expected to judge whether it is pleasant or not but in all circumstances continue to manifest as light.

Joseph continued to manifest as light as he interprets dream to his depressed fellow prisoners. He continued to use his God given gift to bless others even when the circumstances were not favourably to him.

Assuming Joseph did not exhibit his God given gift to bless his fellow prisoners he saw depressed. Assuming Joseph refused to shine as the light of the world in that prison, who would have told Pharaoh that he can interpret dream.

Because you don't know whom God has positioned to be your life lifter, you cannot choose whom or where to manifest as light by using your God given gift.

You may have missed the opportunity of being blessed or promoted because instead of you using your gift to manifest as light you became selfish or self centred and concentrated on your circumstances rather than blessing your world.

More opportunities lies ahead of you to manifest as light so that God can bring you to the position he has prepared for you like Joseph.

If a simple gift of interpretation of dream and wisdom can elevate Joseph from prison to palace, you have equal opportunity to stop looking at your circumstances and manifest as light to the world in order to reach your destiny. **Genesis 40:7-8** "And he asked Pharaoh's officers that were with him in the word of his Lord's house, saying, wherefore look ye so sadly today?

And they said unto him, we have dreamed a dream, and there is no interpreter of it. And Joseph said unto them, do not interpretations belong to God? Tell me them I pray you".

The above concerns of Joseph towards his fellow prisoners caused them to relate their dreams to Joseph. Today we don't have concern or passion for the needs or challengers facing the people of the world.

The gift may be there, but is our concern or passion for the people that enables the gift to manifest. If we must manifest as light, we must develop compassionate attitude towards the people of the world.

Compassion and manifestation of gift of the Holy Spirit characterize the ministry of Jesus Christ and he said I am the light of the world. If we are to be the light of the world as Jesus had said it, we must follow his footstep by being compassionate over the needs of the world.

When Joseph taught he had been forgotten that was when God the owner of the gift stepped in and elevated his as a prime minister of Egypt *Genesis 41:39-40* "And Pharaoh said unto Joseph, for as much as God hath shewed thee all this, there is none so discreet and wise as thou art. Thou shalt be over my house, and according unto thy word shall all my people be ruled. Only in the throne will I be greater than thou".

MOSES
Moses is referred to as the law giver and was credited to have written some of the old testament books. This could not have been achieved if Moses did not accept to be the light of the world when God called him in *Exodus 3:4* "And when the Lord saw that he turned aside to see, God called unto him out of the midst of the bush and said Moses, Moses. And he said here I am".

Moses became an instrument in the hand of God to liberate the children of God from Egypt, the place of bondage.

Today it is required of us to be the Moses of our generation to liberate our people who are in bondage or in darkness.

As many people today are still in bondage of religion, bondage of cultism bondage of self-righteousness and bondage of mammon.

As apostle of the market place, we are the light of God, the Moses of our generation that God had given the responsibility to liberate our people from any form of bondage *Isaiah 61:1* "The Spirit of the Lord God is upon me, because the Lord hath anointed me to preach good tidings unto the meek; he hath sent me to bind up the broken hearted to proclaim liberty to the captives and the opening the prison to them that are bound".

When Moses became the light he fulfilled God's purpose for the children of Israel to bring them to the land God had given to their father Abraham. *Genesis 50:24* "And Joseph said unto his brethren, I die and God will surely visit you, and bring you out of this land unto the Land which he sware to Abraham, to Isaac and to Jacob". Moses accepted to be the light that God used to fulfill the above prophecy. Can you be the next light that God will use to visit and deliver people from any bondage or captivity?

Moses indeed served his generation and served God. Will you be willing to serve God and serve your generation as the light of the world? *Exodus 13:3* "And Moses said unto the people remember this day, in which ye came out from Egypt, out of the house of bondage, for by strength of hand the Lord brought you out from this place".

ESTHER

If Haman had succeeded in his plan to execute the Jews perhaps, there wouldn't have been a modern day Israel. More painful is that the agenda of God may have been truncated because Jesus by God's divine arrangement is to come through the lineage of the Jews.

When darkness wanted to cover the Jews, Esther accepted to be the light that God used to deliver the Jews from extermination by Haman. *Esther 4:16* "Go, gather together all the Jews that are present in Shushan, and fast ye for me, and neither eat nor drink three days, night or day: I also and my maidens will fast likewise, and so will I go in unto the king, which is not according to the law and if I perish, I perish".

Today we have people who belong to other religion that are ready to perish and most times perish for what they belief those who decided to be the Esther of their own religion as suicide bombers.

The people of other religion are not afraid of death and they do have confidence of where they will go if they die, fulfilling the course of their religion.

We who are the children of light are much afraid to die or risk our life or resources for the propagation of the gospel, even when we know or believe that we are going to heaven if we die in righteousness. Esther took risk over her life in order to be the light of the Jews.

Are we ready to take risk of our life, our resources in other to be the light of the world? Esther fulfill her assignment as the light of the world see *Esther 7:3-4* "Then Esther the queen answered and said if I have found favour in thy sight, O king and if it please the king, let my life be given me at my petition, and my people at my request; for we are sold, I and my people, to be destroyed, to be slain and to perish. But if we had been sold for bondmen and bondwomen, I had held my tongue, although the enemy could not countervail the king's damage".

Today we have an enemy that is still working more than Haman whose task is to steal, kill and destroy.

But just like Esther have found favour before the king. We have found favour before the king of kings to deliver our people, our generation from the hands of the enemy that has come to steal, kill and destroy their lives.

Go ahead and plead the cause of the captives, God is all ears to hear our petition and save all that are in bondage.

DAVID

This is the man after God's own heart. It means that David started chasing after God and finally entrenched himself in the heart of God. This he achieved by the things he did.

David saw an uncircumcised Philistine defying the armies of the living God and could not tolerate such shame and decided to be the light of the children of Israel. *1Samuel 17:36* "Thy servant slew both the lion and the bear and this uncircumcised Philistine shall be as one of them, seeing he hath defied the armies of the living God."

Nation of Israel was in bondage of fear of Goliath *1Samuel 17:24* "And all the men of Israel when they saw the man, fled from him and were sore afraid".

Today's world many men are afraid of the future, afraid of where the next meal will be coming from.

The emergency of diseases like cancer, diabetes, Ebola, Zika virus and others have made the people of the world in constant fear and need an apostle of the market place that will shine as light and bring healings and divine health for them.

There are wars, violence, shootings and terrorism everywhere in the world. All these act is perpetrated by the same enemy. We need men that will act like David and bring this enemies of mankind down by confronting them and setting the people of the world free.

PAUL

The word of God is a light to the world ***Psalm. 119:105, 130*** "Thy word is a lamp unto my feet, and a light unto my path. The entrance of thy words giveth light; it giveth understanding unto the simple"

Paul is known to have encountered the great light during his time of conversion ***Acts 9:3*** "And as he journeyed, he came near Damascus and suddenly there shined round about him a light from heaven".

After Paul's conversion, the instruction given to him was to be an apostle in the market place Act. 9:15 "But the Lord said unto him, go thy way, for he is a chosen vessel unto me, to bear my name before the Gentiles, kings and the children of Israel".

Paul became a light to the world as an apostle of the market place. Paul wrote the highest number of books of the bible. Through his writing the word of God, the light of God spread to the entire world.

All these are few examples of how men and women in diverse ways became the light of the world.

We are enjoined by the word of God to be the light of the world see Isa. 61:1-7.

www.ingramcontent.com/pod-product-compliance
Lightning Source LLC
Chambersburg PA
CBHW031623210526
45464CB00004B/1719